M000195701

American Empire at the Turn of the Twentieth Century

A Brief History with Documents

Kristin L. Hoganson

University of Illinois, Urbana-Champaign

bedford/st.martin's
Macmillan Learning

Boston | New York

For Bedford/St. Martin's

Vice President, Editorial, Macmillan Learning Humanities: Edwin Hill
Publisher for History: Michael Rosenberg
Senior Executive Editor for History: William J. Lombardo
Director of Development for History: Jane Knetzger
Senior Developmental Editor: Leah R. Strauss
Editorial Assistant: Alexandra DeConti
History Marketing Manager: Melissa Famiglietti
Production Editor: Lidia MacDonald-Carr
Production Supervisor: Robert Cherry
Director of Rights and Permissions: Hilary Newman
Permissions Associate: Michael McCarty
Permissions Manager: Kalina Ingham
Cover Design: William Boardman
Cover Photo: (Front cover) Library of Congress, Prints & Photographs Division,
   Reproduction number LC-USZC4-7934 (color film copy transparency); LC-USZ62-7626
   (b&w film copy neg.); (back cover) Kristin L. Hoganson
Project Management: Books By Design, Inc.
Cartographer: Mapping Specialists, Ltd.
Composition: Achorn International, Inc.
Printing and Binding: LSC Communications

1   0   9   8   7   6
f   e   d   c   b   a

For information, write: Bedford/St. Martin's, 75 Arlington Street, Boston, MA 02116
   (617-399-4000)

ISBN 978-0-312-67705-3

Acknowledgments

*Acknowledgments and copyrights appear on the same page as the text and art selections they
cover; these acknowledgments and copyrights constitute an extension of the copyright page.*

At the time of publication all Internet URLs published in this text were found to
accurately link to their intended Web site. If you do find a broken link, please forward
the information to history@macmillan.com so that it can be corrected for the next
printing.

To the students, teachers, and research team who brought this book into being and to the authors of my favorite documents herein, who once again show the relevance of history and its unending capacity to move us

Foreword

The Bedford Series in History and Culture is designed so that readers can study the past as historians do.

The historian's first task is finding the evidence. Documents, letters, memoirs, interviews, pictures, movies, novels, or poems can provide facts and clues. Then the historian questions and compares the sources. There is more to do than in a courtroom, for hearsay evidence is welcome, and the historian is usually looking for answers beyond act and motive. Different views of an event may be as important as a single verdict. How a story is told may yield as much information as what it says.

Along the way the historian seeks help from other historians and perhaps from specialists in other disciplines. Finally, it is time to write, to decide on an interpretation and how to arrange the evidence for readers.

Each book in this series contains an important historical document or group of documents, each document a witness from the past and open to interpretation in different ways. The documents are combined with some element of historical narrative—an introduction or a biographical essay, for example—that provides students with an analysis of the primary source material and important background information about the world in which it was produced.

Each book in the series focuses on a specific topic within a specific historical period. Each provides a basis for lively thought and discussion about several aspects of the topic and the historian's role. Each is short enough (and inexpensive enough) to be a reasonable one-week assignment in a college course. Whether as classroom or personal reading, each book in the series provides firsthand experience of the challenge—and fun—of discovering, recreating, and interpreting the past.

Lynn Hunt
David W. Blight
Bonnie G. Smith

Foreword

Preface

The course of American empire around 1898 left a lasting mark on the geographic extent of the United States, the demographic composition of the American people, and the uneven allocation of political rights across U.S. states and territories. The echoes of 1898 still reverberate in the global reach of the United States, its exercise of military force beyond its own borders, and its network of bases, alliances, and affiliations. Trade, capital flows, development policies, missionary endeavors, human migration, and global awareness—all have deep imperial roots, as revealed by the documents in this volume.

To fully comprehend how the United States became a global power, we need to engage with histories of empire. Studying the history of American empire reveals ways that relations with other peoples have shaped seemingly domestic histories. And just as importantly, the lens of empire can help us understand the histories of those drawn into the U.S. sphere and the foundations of the global system we inhabit today.

Once, in a workshop for K–12 teachers, a keen participant asked me about the relevance of American empire, given its absence in the set curriculum. The place was Worcester, Massachusetts. I asked how many of the teachers in the room had Cuban American students in their classes. Every hand went up. Filipino American? Ditto. Puerto Rican? Everyone. The same for students with Dominican, Mexican, Native American, Chinese, and Haitian ancestry. The relevance of this topic could be seen in every classroom in the district. The histories revealed by these documents shape family stories across the United States and meaningful historical memories far from U.S. shores.

To be sure, textbooks have long covered the Spanish-Cuban-American War and the U.S.-Philippine War. In recent years, they have devoted more attention to topics such as the annexation of Hawai'i and Puerto Rico and the military occupations that supposedly turned the Caribbean into an American lake. This volume supplements the growing coverage of American empire around 1898 by connecting political and military histories to cultural and economic histories. It goes beyond the typical cast of U.S. political and military leaders to incorporate a broader range of perspectives. It draws attention to the global imperial system that shaped American outlooks and actions. And it situates the military interventions and annexations of 1898 in a wider context—stretching back to earlier policies toward Native Americans and forward to interventions in places like Panama and Haiti. This more integrated approach can help readers appreciate the extent of U.S. imperial reach around the turn of the twentieth century, the problems that it posed, the range of debates that it generated, and the linkages and patterns that emerged across space and time.

The book begins with an interpretive essay that sets up the documents that follow. The essay introduces readers to key events, places, people, and debates. It places the history of American empire in a global history framework and draws attention to major themes extending across time and place. The headings that break up this essay enable it to be read in sections, and they provide easy reference to particular topics.

The forty-eight documents gathered in this collection are clustered by topic. Yet the documents also speak to each other outside of their specific clusters. The documents justifying U.S. policies in the Philippines, for example, can be fruitfully read against those that critique it. The documents under the heading "Colonial Governance" connect to the documents on the United States in an age of empire, co-opting the Cuban Revolution, military conduct, and race making in colonial contexts. This latter topic surfaces throughout the book, as do economic concerns, military matters, discussions of democracy, and attentiveness to other empires.

Each document is prefaced by a short stage-setting headnote. Gloss notes explain obscure terms. The brief chronology at the end of the book lists key events and dates. The discussion questions will help students dive into the issues raised by the documents. Readers seeking more information can consult the bibliography, arranged by topic; those with specific interests can consult the index.

A NOTE ABOUT THE TEXT

I have left the spellings as found in the original documents with the exception of misspellings that are clearly typesetting errors. I use *Hawaii* to refer to the state of that name. But I refer to the island chain as the

Hawai'ian Islands and the big island as Hawai'i. These spellings have emerged from a push for greater recognition of native Hawai'ian culture and awareness of the colonial pasts that this book helps bring to light.

ACKNOWLEDGMENTS

This book emerged from a series of teaching workshops sponsored by the Teaching American History Program (funded by the National Endowment for the Humanities), the Newberry Library, the Chicago History Fair, the American Antiquarian Society, and several school districts in Illinois and Massachusetts. Many thanks to the organizers—especially Brodie Austin, Crystal Johnson, Robert Johnston, John McClymer, Rachel Rooney, and Amy Sopcak-Joseph—and the participants for planting the seed.

I am also indebted to my students at the University of Illinois, Urbana-Champaign, and the Ludwig-Maximilians-Universität in Munich (where I taught as a visiting Fulbright professor) for testing many more documents than appear here. Particular thanks are due to the following students, whose research and "expert witness testimony" helped shape this collection: Alex Anderson, Adrian Barajas, Patrick Clark, Harsha Eswarappa, Alec Heist, Simon Holstein, Mike Jensen, Doug Johnson, Jeremy Karpenski, Shawn Ledbetter, Nora Lucas, Adam Matos, John Moreland, Steve Ross, Joshua Scott, Matt Seeberg, Eileen Simon, Justin Smith, Matt Sugrue, XiXi Tian, William Wang, John Watters, Jamieson Westergaard, and James Zenn (all at Illinois) and Munich students Florian Aß, Maciej Cerynger, Gesine Groke, Sabine Harderer, Michael Kull, Nataliya Matveeva, Emily McCollum, Marcel Müller, Niklas Nau, Leonardo Peruzzi, Maximilian Reimann, and Felix Steffan.

My debts extend to several resourceful, insightful, and capable research assistants: Nick Wozniak, Julie Laut, Josh Levy, and Matt Harshman. They did substantial work on this volume, extending well beyond library legwork.

Catherine Cocks, Augusto Espiritu, Scott Gurman, Daniel Immerwahr, Paul Kramer, Jana K. Lipman, Sarah D. Manekin, Alex M. (Sasha) Mobley, Michael Salman, Ellen Tillman, and Steve Tuffnell graciously offered bibliographic and other guidance. Carol Rose Parker, Tricia Warfield, and Brooke Bear provided essential office support. Among the many librarians who enabled this book, Kathryn Danner, Paula Carns, Charles Bjork, and Paul Gatz of the University of Illinois merit special thanks. Thoughtful commentary by Thomas Borstelmann, University of

Nebraska–Lincoln; Benjamin Coates, Wake Forest University; David Dzurec, University of Scranton; Anne L. Foster, Indiana State University; Stephen R. Porter, University of Cincinnati; William Woodward, Seattle Pacific University; and Thomas W. Zeiler, University of Colorado Boulder, made this a far better book.

Bill Lombardo, Senior Executive Editor, and Leah Strauss, Senior Development Editor, of Bedford/St. Martin's also deserve warm mention, as do Publisher Michael Rosenberg, Director of Development Jane Knetzger, History Marketing Manager Melissa Famiglietti, Editorial Assistant Alexandra DeConti, Production Editor Lidia MacDonald-Carr, Cover Designer William Boardman, Copyeditor Judith Riotto, and Production Coordinator Nancy Benjamin of Books By Design. My most heartfelt gratitude goes to the irrepressible Jerry, Annemily, and Edith Frances, and, as always, Charles.

Kristin L. Hoganson

Contents

PART TWO

The Documents   33

Maps and Illustrations

PART ONE

Introduction:
The United States in an
Age of Empire

AMERICAN EMPIRE

With its thirteen stripes and fifty stars, the American flag evokes the history of a nation that grew from founding colonies to a larger union of states. In addition to flying over the U.S. Capitol in the District of Columbia and each of the nation's statehouses, it flies, often alongside other flags, on U.S. Indian reservations, in the territories of American Samoa, Guam, and the U.S. Virgin Islands, and in the commonwealths (which have more political autonomy than territories) of Puerto Rico and the Northern Mariana Islands. Its symbolic reach extends over an assortment of smaller, largely unpopulated islands in the Caribbean and Pacific.

The American flag is likewise found on the many U.S. bases and other military installations across the globe. A disproportionately high number of military personnel serving under the American flag during deployments in Iraq and Afghanistan hailed from the Pacific islands of Palau, the Federated States of Micronesia, and the Republic of the Marshall Islands, all of which have entered into Compacts of Free Association with the United States. Millions of U.S. citizens who salute the Stars and Stripes can trace their ancestors back to places where the American flag once heralded the landing of U.S. troops, where its presence signaled a shift in borders or set in motion significant migration to the United States.

The American flag serves as the paramount symbol of the nation. Yet the journey from thirteen stripes to fifty stars and the even wider reach of this flag also reveal histories of empire. In its strict sense, the term *empire* refers to a nation that has expanded its scope to rule other people and territory on unequal terms. In a more general sense, the term *imperial* refers to political relationships characterized by vast disparities in power, violence or the threat of violence, varying degrees of autonomy, and differentiated rights dependent on geography and population group. As these definitions suggest, the word *imperialism* can be applied to a wide range of relationships. It might imply *settler colonialism*—meaning the displacement of indigenous people by newcomers under the aegis of a more powerful state.[1] It can refer to *territorial acquisition* without a huge influx of settlers or *indirect rule* through coercion, intimidation, reliance on collaborators, and financial control. The phrases *economic imperialism* and *cultural imperialism* further broaden the analytic frame by highlighting forms of domination and subordination that, though entangled with state power, have their own particular sources and dynamics.

Histories of empire encompass relationships driven by compulsion as well as ones in which cultural attraction figures largely. These histories can be larger than national histories insofar as they refer to hierarchies that extend beyond the nation and connections across vast systems, yet we can also find evidence of empire on smaller scales: in legislatures, battlefields, homes, hospitals, schools, plantations, and marketplaces. To understand the nature of American empire, we have to consider not only government officials and military personnel, but also anticolonial activists, missionaries, and canal diggers; not only political, military, and economic matters, but also ideology and culture. In trying to determine who benefitted and who lost out, and how and why, we need to stay alert to the possibility that class, gender, race, ethnicity, and political affiliation could unite people across boundaries while dividing them within.

Opening up American history so that it encompasses empire can help us understand the making of the American people and the complexities of American democracy, including why the residents of Puerto Rico and other U.S. territories, though U.S. citizens (with the exception of the Samoans, some of whom are currently pressing to change their "noncitizen national" status to citizenship), send only nonvoting delegates to the House of Representatives and no delegates to the U.S. Senate; why they participate in the presidential primary process but not the final elections; and why laws passed by their territorial governments can be nullified by the U.S. Congress. An imperial framework can help us understand the histories of people and places drawn into the orbit of U.S. power. Just as importantly, the analytic lens of imperialism provides valuable insights into the scope and nature of U.S. power and the historical roots of contemporary globalization.

THE IMPERIAL WORLD SYSTEM

The world has known various forms of empire since long before the Romans. The expansion of European empires into the Americas starting in 1492 knit Atlantic, Pacific, and Indian Ocean holdings into an interconnected world system over the next few centuries. Although not all empires emanated from Europe—as seen, for example, in the cases of the Ottoman, Inca, Chinese, Japanese, and Comanche empires—European powers soon became leading holders of overseas (as opposed to land-based) empires. Further European expansion into Asia, the Pacific islands, the Middle East, and Africa meant that upon the outbreak of World War I in 1914, European colonists and their descendants governed the Americas, nearly all of Africa, and much of Asia and the Pacific, stretching from India to Vietnam, Indonesia, the Philippines, and New Zealand. The British Empire was by far the most colossal; maps that shaded a quarter of the world's inhabited lands as British still failed to capture the full extent of Britain's naval and financial might.[2] (See Map 1.)

Even as imperial transportation and communication networks drew the world closer together, imperial policies led to new divisions of wealth and power. Whereas in 1880, per capita income in the European imperial powers was about double that in their overseas colonies, by 1913, it was three times greater and rising.[3] Recognizing the unsurpassed reach of European states from the "scramble for Africa" that kicked off in the 1880s to the traumas of World War I, historians have labeled this period an age of empire. Though useful markers, these starting and ending dates obscure longer-term continuities, stretching forward in time as well as back. Despite the U.S., Haitian, and Latin American independence movements of the late eighteenth and early nineteenth centuries and vigorous anticolonial sentiments expressed across the colonized world, the great wave of decolonization did not come until after World War II.

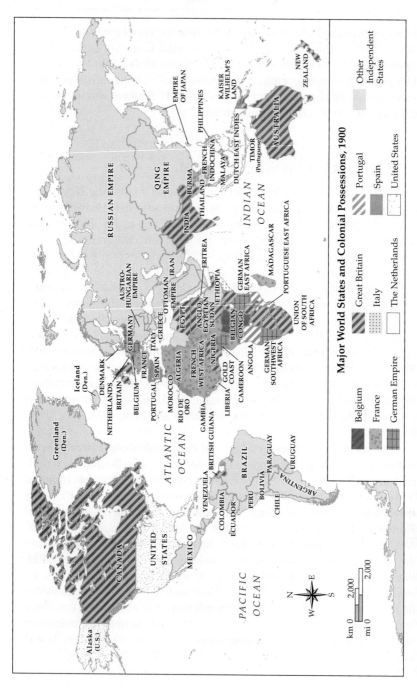

Map 1. *The Imperial World System on the Eve of World War I, 1914*

4

1898 IN THE LARGER SWEEP OF TIME

Anti-imperialist currents have threaded through U.S. history since the nation's inception in a war for independence. Evidence of anti-imperialist convictions can be found in President James Monroe's 1823 statement against European colonization of independent Latin American republics, the 1899 Open Door Notes (which demanded an end to imperial preferences in the China trade), and President Woodrow Wilson's calls for national self-determination for European peoples. Yet even these examples of anti-imperialist leanings reveal imperial currents. The Monroe Doctrine also provided rhetorical firepower to those who advocated U.S. expansion and hemispheric supremacy. The Open Door Notes demanded access, not an end to empire, and U.S. policymakers did not call for open doors quite so loudly when it came to their own spheres of influence. Wilson's disregard for the rights of people of color likewise reveals countervailing commitments to empire.[4]

The most enduring opposition to U.S. imperialism can be found in the histories of Native American peoples who resisted U.S. expansion into their lands. Like settler colonists in Russian Central Asia, Argentina, Canada, New Zealand, Australia, South Africa, and Brazil, U.S. settlers (some accompanied, unwillingly, by slaves) displaced, confined, and subjected the people they encountered.[5] The United States also gained a substantial amount of territory from Mexico following the Mexican-American War of 1846–1848. Stemming from the U.S. annexation of Texas, a former Mexican state with a disputed southern boundary, the war resulted in the cession of about 525,000 square miles of territory claimed by Mexico, stretching from Texas to California. In addition to making many Mexican nationals residents of the United States, the shift in boundaries also extended claims of U.S. sovereignty over Comanche, Pueblo, Apache, Navajo, Ute, and other Native American peoples.[6] Military conflict between the United States and Native American nations persisted through the massacre of about three hundred Lakota Sioux at Wounded Knee, South Dakota, in 1890. This massacre marked the close of the U.S. Indian Wars, though indigenous peoples continued to struggle for autonomy, land, and rights.[7]

The so-called Manifest Destiny expansion of the mid-nineteenth century was not the only form of U.S. imperialism with lasting legacies. The African colonization movement, which took off in 1816 with the formation of the American Colonization Society, provided another model for expansion. Unable to envision a mixed-race republic that would offer freedom and equality to all its members, many colonizationists regarded the relocation of African Americans to Liberia as an emancipatory program that would save the United States from a large population of free black people as well as from the scourge of slavery. Although some African Americans bitterly denounced the racist reasons for supporting colonization, others saw relocation to Liberia as a means to achieve freedom and greater opportunities (Document 44). Black and white supporters alike saw another benefit in colonization: the uplift of native Africans. Failing to appreciate that West African peoples might resent African Americans as encroachers, colonization supporters envisioned Liberia as a potential client state. This nineteenth-century model, mixing settler colonialism and informal control of a nominally sovereign state, was as important a precedent for later policies and practices as continental expansion.[8]

Although the African colonization movement had some U.S. government backing in the form of naval appropriations, it fit into a larger pattern of nongovernmental endeavors that expanded U.S. reach in the antebellum period. Whalers, merchant vessels, and illicit slave ships plied the oceans of the world, with stops in European colonial outposts and the onetime colonies of Latin America to reprovision and to trade. Missionaries also crossed the seas en route to "heathen lands," many of them newly accessible due to European colonial expansion. Southern slaveholders invested in and looked to annex the Caribbean islands that had resisted emancipation. A New York company, backed by its own private police force, completed the world's first transcontinental railroad in 1855 across the Isthmus of Panama, to speed access to the goldfields of California. Armed individuals known as filibusters went a step farther by invading countries such as Mexico and Nicaragua, in many cases with annexationist ambitions and in violation of U.S. policies.[9]

Although the private sector did not always march in lockstep with the U.S. government, commercial ambitions sparked government action, and assertive government policies enabled greater access. In 1853, Commodore Matthew Perry sailed into Tokyo Bay backed by a fleet of warships to demand that Japan open its ports to U.S. vessels. Japanese officials acceded to Perry's demands in the 1854 Treaty of Kanagawa. Such assertion surfaced again in the U.S. military action in Korea in 1871. A U.S. naval expedition charged with negotiating a pro-trade treaty drew fire upon approaching a sensitive fort. Abandoning their original mission, the U.S. officers opted for retaliation, leaving at least 250 Koreans dead. This clash was the largest use of overseas U.S. military force between the Mexican-American War of 1846–1848 and the war against Spain in 1898.[10]

Another manifestation of U.S. power in the Pacific and East Asia can be glimpsed in the legal practice known as extraterritoriality. Established by treaty, extraterritoriality extended U.S. jurisdiction to U.S. nationals living and working overseas. Thus if a U.S. sailor or merchant were to commit a crime while living in Canton, it would be the U.S. consul rather than local officials who would hear the case and determine the punishment. The United States signed its first such treaty in 1844, with the Qing Empire in China. Subsequent treaties followed with Borneo (1850), Siam (1856), Japan (1857), Samoa (1878), Korea (1882), and Tonga (1886). Unlike earlier treaties that granted some extraterritorial privileges in the Muslim states of North Africa, none of these treaties were reciprocal. Chinese men and women living in the United States not only were subject to U.S. rule but were discriminated against by U.S. law, as were their U.S.-born descendants.[11]

The attitudes that underlay these treaties also accompanied the flood of U.S. settlers into lands claimed by Native Americans and Mexicans. The acquisition of new territory stalled during the Civil War, but Secretary of State William Henry Seward made up for that in 1867 with the purchase of Alaska from the Russian Empire. Though not contiguous to the rest of the United States, Alaska might soon be, reasoned Seward, for it would usher in the annexation of the British Dominion of Canada. Seward also acquired the uninhabited Midway Islands—about two miles square—in the center of the Pacific, and he endorsed the annexation of various guano islands (small Caribbean and Pacific outcroppings mined for their nitrogen-rich bird droppings). Seward made a bid to annex the Dominican Republic, as did his successor under President Ulysses S. Grant, but the Senate refused to ratify the necessary treaties, in part due to concerns about incorporating so many people of color into the United States (Document 1).[12]

Following the Civil War, Union efforts to reconstruct and reincorporate the secessionist states established another important precedent for later occupations. Additional continuities over time can be seen in the U.S. officer corps. Many of the officers who led the campaigns of 1898 had honed their skills fighting Native Americans in the U.S. West, and some of the most senior had first been initiated into the military during the Civil War. The lasting legacies of the Civil War can also be seen in the claims that overseas interventions would reknit the nation by bringing Union blue and Confederate gray together on the field of battle.[13]

As the great powers competed for trading posts, coaling stations, and colonies, some political economists began to wonder if the vast resources and markets within the United States would suffice in a world of massive empires. Historian Frederick Jackson Turner's 1893 essay on the closing of the frontier prompted further interest in overseas colonies. Although many Irish Americans continued to loathe the British Empire due to its ongoing rule over Ireland, increasing references to Anglo-Saxon brotherhood and the civilizing mission reveal a sense of common cause with Britain and the Europe-dominated imperial order it exemplified (Documents 3 and 4).[14]

EXPANDING INTERESTS

In the late nineteenth century, the United States emerged as a world economic power. The nearly twenty million workers who came to the United States between 1870 and 1910 contributed to the nation's rising industrial might. About a third of these workers stayed only a few years before returning home, where they shifted from being the targets of Americanizing ambitions to proponents of cultural and economic Americanization. The tremendous human mobility of the late nineteenth century fueled efforts to control the nation's borders, which had been largely open for most of the nineteenth century. The 1882 Chinese Exclusion Act that denied entry to Chinese workers (though not to students, merchants, or professionals) began a new regulatory era.[15]

Even as the U.S. government sought to limit entry to the United States via immigration restriction and high tariffs, it sought unimpeded access to the rest of the world for its citizens and goods. In a reversal of earlier patterns, it became a net exporting nation in 1874, a trend that continued with only a few exceptions until the current trade deficit era began in 1971. The majority of U.S. exports had historically been agricultural goods, but manufactured products gained ground in the 1880s. Companies like McCormick Harvester, Singer Sewing Machine, H. J. Heinz, and Standard Oil began to market their products not only to Europe and Canada but wider afield as well. The drive for overseas markets became all the more pressing due to an economic slump starting in 1873. Concerns that the domestic market would not be able to absorb the tremendous domestic productive capacity led many farmers and manufacturers to see the solution to hard times in foreign buyers, especially in the potentially vast yet largely untapped China market.[16]

Although U.S. businesses were quicker to market their products overseas than to invest in overseas production of raw materials and goods, such investments rose in the late nineteenth century. Frustrated by protective policies that restricted their investments in European colonies,

U.S. companies looked elsewhere for opportunity. They found much of it in Mexico, which attracted more direct U.S. investment than any other country during the pro-investment regime of Porfirio Díaz (in power from 1877 to 1910, though with a puppet in the presidency from 1880 to 1884). The Guggenheim brothers, Phelps Dodge Corporation, and other well-capitalized investors purchased mines and built smelters. Railroad barons laid tracks, cattle kings purchased ranches, and oil magnates dug wells (Document 46).[17] Canada also attracted investment capital, surpassing Mexico by 1914. The Caribbean drew more modest amounts of capital, much of it in sugar and banana plantations (Document 48).[18]

Many businessmen objected to government spending, believing in the self-regulating power of the market. However, a vocal cluster demanded more consular officers to gather commercial information and press for access and extraterritorial privileges, a plausible threat of ground troops to secure overseas investments, a stronger navy to protect U.S. merchants, and coaling stations to enable U.S. ships to cross the wide expanses of the Pacific. Heeding such calls, the United States jumped into a rivalry with Germany and Britain over influence in Samoa, signing a treaty in 1878 granting it Pago Pago Harbor as a naval station.[19] (See Map 2.) Alfred Thayer Mahan significantly advanced the case for naval building in *The Influence of Sea Power upon History*, published in 1890. Increased expenditures enabled the U.S. Navy to ascend in world rankings, to the seventh most powerful by 1893.[20]

THE GOLDEN AGE OF MISSIONS

In conjunction with its expanding commercial and military footprint, the United States established a greater overseas cultural presence in this period. So many missionaries set forth for "heathen" lands between 1880 and 1920 that these years have been called a golden age of missionary enterprise. Chief among the missionaries' destinations were the Near East—including Turkey and North Africa—and the Far East, especially China. In their many reports and fund-raising appeals, missionaries emphasized their educational and medical contributions as well as their role in bringing salvation to non-Christians (Document 8). Most Americans viewed such endeavors positively, as evidence that their nation was a force for good in the world.[21] While sometimes claiming to be opponents of empire—as benevolent rather than rapacious, as voluntaristic rather than coercive—missionaries often relied on imperial power for access. Their efforts to effect social and cultural change sometimes generated local backlashes, as in the Boxer Uprising in China (1899–1901). When attacked, missionaries called for military protection and government support for their compensation claims (Document 11).[22]

The role of missionaries as an opening wedge for other forms of involvement can be seen in Hawai'i. From roughly 1825 to 1850, U.S. missionaries shifted Hawai'ian sovereignty from the high chiefs—who ruled according to sacred laws, justifying their power through hereditary rank and religious authority—to the people, through a written constitution, elected legislature, and common law. Though democratic in principle, this system was oligarchic in practice, for it restricted voting to men of property, among them, sons of missionaries. Along with other foreigners who had invested in plantations, these men staged a coup in 1893 that took power from Queen Liliuokalani (also spelled Lili'uokalani) (Document 9). They then pressed for annexation to their leading export market, the United States. President Grover Cleveland thwarted this demand, but only temporarily. In 1898, the sugar barons' economic interests aligned with the U.S. interest in Pacific coaling stations, and Hawai'i became a U.S. territory, with statehood eventually following in 1959.[23]

CRISIS IN CUBA

Once the leader in American colonization, Spain lost most of its empire as a result of the Latin American independence movements from 1808 to 1826. It managed to hang on to Cuba, the "ever-faithful isle," because of slavery. With an economy that rested largely on sugar production, Cuban planters relied on African-origin slaves to do most of the hard work of sugarcane production and on Spanish military power to keep their unfree labor force in subjection. Although slavery tied most Cuban planters to the Spanish Empire, some white Cubans joined with Afro-Cubans (both slave and free) to fight for independence in the Ten Years' War (1868–1878) and the subsequent Little War (1879–1880). The revolutionaries failed in these bids for national independence, but their efforts did lead to emancipation by 1886. Yet even this advance failed to win the allegiance of Afro-Cubans, by then about a third of the island's population, because Spain did not grant universal manhood suffrage or endorse racial equality.[24]

The conflict in Cuba caused tens of thousands of Cubans to depart for the United States. Many of these expatriates supported independence, and they worked through a group known as the Cuban Junta to build support for the Cuban cause. Beyond the reach of Spanish officials, expatriate members of the Cuban Revolutionary Party such as Tomás Estrada Palma and Gonzalo de Quesada continued the struggle to free Cuba from Spanish rule.[25]

Economic hard times helped the revolutionary cause. The first two wars for independence hit Cuban sugar estates hard. Making things worse, Cuban planters had to contend with expanding sugarcane cultivation in places like Louisiana and Hawaii and the rise of the sugar beet. As world sugar prices fell, the United States passed the 1894 Wilson-Gorman Tariff Act. The restrictive duties included in this act curtailed Cuban exports to the U.S. market, which had absorbed about 94 percent of Cuban sugar in the 1880s. Spain's decision to levy higher taxes on Cuban planters even in the midst of economic crisis helped spark a third war for independence, starting in 1895 (Document 12).[26]

Despite transporting over 190,000 soldiers to Cuba—then the largest army ever sent to fight a colonial war—Spain could not subdue the rebellion. Cuban military leaders recognized that the path to success was through attrition, not major battlefield encounters. With this in mind, they waged a guerrilla war in the countryside, leaving tropical diseases to fell a fifth of the Spanish army, composed largely of poor conscripts. In 1896, the Spanish general Valeriano Weyler, nicknamed "The Butcher" in the United States, interned about half a million rural villagers in camps to prevent them from aiding the insurgents. The consequence, more widely reported by the U.S. press than the results of the insurgents' torches, was disease, starvation, and death (Document 13).[27]

After three years of fighting, the Cuban forces had exhausted the Spanish army, yet the Spanish forces, still in control of the towns, refused to pull out. Following several riots in Havana in January 1898, the U.S. consul Fitzhugh Lee requested a warship be sent to Havana to protect the U.S. community there. The U.S. Navy sent the *Maine*. The battleship blew up and sank on the night of February 15, with a loss of 266 lives. The Navy convened a court of inquiry, which blamed the incident on a mine. Although the commission had no evidence proving Spanish responsibility, the U.S. media blamed Spain. (Later investigations suggest that the fault lay with a fire in the coal supply, located next to the ammunition magazine.) In the male-dominated political system of the time—a system that venerated military service, fighting spirit, and fraternal loyalty—it seemed politically suicidal not to avenge the dead sailors through war. Stung by charges that he lacked the manly fortitude to lead the nation into war, that he had in the words of Theodore Roosevelt, "no more backbone than a chocolate éclair," President

William McKinley asked Congress for the authority to intervene in Cuba. Congress enthusiastically complied.[28]

WHY DID THE UNITED STATES INTERVENE IN THE CUBAN-SPANISH WAR?

The *Maine* explosion provided the immediate pretext for the U.S. intervention in Cuba, but the calls for action that preceded the disaster show that the *Maine* alone does not fully explain the U.S. entry into the Cuban-Spanish War. Investors—with about $50 million worth of property in Cuba in 1895—had long agitated for intervention in the war, as did those who had purchased Cuban bonds (offered to enable arms purchases).[29] Although the commercial press contained plenty of antiwar articles, a range of individuals urged war for economic reasons.[30]

Another set of explanations focuses on humanitarian motives. This line of thought emphasizes the role of the sensationalist "yellow press" (named after the dress color of a popular cartoon character), which ran front-page stories on Spanish atrocities in Cuba. Less inflammatory newspapers also adhered to the narrative of Spanish villainy and Cuban victimization, thereby overlooking the Cuban guerrillas' brutal tactics.[31]

A third set of explanations pertains to territorial and strategic calculations. From the early years of the American republic, annexationists— particularly proslavery Southerners—had kept an eye on Cuba. By the 1890s, naval theorists urged the acquisition of Caribbean bases that could protect a coveted Central American canal from European rivals. Such territorial and strategic calculations came to a head with the realization that the multiracial coalition of Cuban nationalists had basically won its war against Spain. The only way the United States could prevent Cuban independence was through intervention.[32]

The pervasive racism of the era incited the opposition to Cuban independence. By the 1890s, the United States had retreated from Reconstruction-era efforts to achieve a multiracial democracy. This was a time notable for the entrenchment of race-based suffrage, Jim Crow social practices, and lynchings to enforce white supremacy. The white Americans who feared African American participation in U.S. politics were no more enthusiastic about Cuban self-determination.[33] Racism did not necessarily lead to annexationist ambitions—as seen in arguments against acquiring the Dominican Republic—but it did undergird talk of tutelage and the need for oversight.

Adding to this mix of motives and conditions was the sense among many Americans—labeled jingoes at the time—that war itself, for whatever reason, might benefit American men by building the kind of martial character associated with Civil War veterans and frontiersmen. As Theodore Roosevelt put it in 1897: "I should welcome almost any war, for I think this country needs one" (Document 25).[34]

U.S. INTERVENTION IN CUBA

In the initial war plan, the U.S. Navy would blockade Cuba until the Spanish had been starved into submission, at which point a small contingent of U.S. Army regulars would land. But state militias clamored so loudly to join the fight that President McKinley called for 200,000 volunteers and an increase in the regular army. Many of these recruits spent the war in overcrowded southern camps, where they suffered from inedible rations (disparaged as "embalmed beef") and sickening sanitary conditions.[35]

The plan to bring the overweening naval power of the United States to bear on Spain hit a glitch when one of its lead vessels, the *Oregon*, took sixty-six days to travel from San Francisco around Cape Horn to Cuba. The long voyage helped demonstrate the value of a canal through the Isthmus of Panama. Notwithstanding such delays, the U.S. fleet bottled up Spain's four leading vessels in Santiago Harbor. When they made a break for the ocean, the U.S. ships destroyed them. The establishment of U.S. naval supremacy meant Spain had no way to provision its forces in Cuba. A defeat on land was sure to follow.[36]

Even as the naval battle raged, U.S. troops were fighting their way toward Santiago over land.[37] Although he made the questionable decision to lead his men directly up Kettle Hill into Spanish gunfire, Colonel Theodore Roosevelt of the First U.S. Volunteer Cavalry (popularly known as the Rough Riders, after an act in a Wild West show) trumpeted his successes so effectively that he emerged a national hero (Documents 18 and 19). Fewer than four hundred U.S. servicemen died in battle, about five thousand from disease.[38]

Upon intervening in the Cuban-Spanish War, the United States promised in a resolution known as the Teller Amendment (named after Senator Henry M. Teller) that it supported Cuban independence (Document 16). But the U.S. military enraged Cuban leaders by excluding them from the negotiations that brought the fighting to a close and from the surrender of Santiago. Such exclusionary acts stemmed from disparaging views of the Cuban revolutionaries. Whereas, prior to the U.S. intervention, there had been a great deal of favorable press coverage of the Cuban Revolution, the tenor of U.S. reports quickly changed. Few dispatches acknowledged that Cuban forces had cleared the beaches for the U.S. landing and had cut off supplies to the Spanish forces. Instead, white U.S. soldiers reported that Cuban forces were nowhere to be found, that instead of teeming with heroic George Washingtons, Cuba was full of cowardly shirkers who lacked the manly character necessary for self-government.[39]

If, prior to the war, Cuban poverty appeared to be part and parcel of the same problems besetting the United States, after the U.S. intervention, newspapers depicted Cuba as a place apart. Failing to appreciate the extent to which years of fighting had desolated the island, American observers wrote Cuba off as an undeveloped and nonwhite country ill-suited for incorporation into the United States. In a decision redolent of slavery, the U.S. commander in Cuba, General Leonard Wood, made violators of his civic code subject to public whippings. The U.S. military played a major role in promoting segregationist practices on the island.[40]

In 1901, Senator Orville Platt of Connecticut introduced an amendment to an Army appropriation bill that countered the Teller Amendment's statements on Cuban independence. The Platt Amendment stipulated that the United States would get a base at Guantánamo, Cuba, and that the United States would have the right to intervene in Cuban affairs to preserve a republican government. News of the amendment sparked anti-U.S. demonstrations across the island. Secretary of War Elihu Root demanded that Cuban leaders incorporate the Platt Amendment into the Cuban constitution, and with their hopes of any independence at stake, they did (Document 17).[41]

Following the provisions of the new constitution, the Cuban electorate chose Tomás Estrada Palma, a leader of the Ten Years' War, as the nation's president. Estrada was a naturalized U.S. citizen, having lived abroad for nearly thirty years. His long exile made him more acceptable to U.S. leaders, and it helped him attract support from competing political factions in Cuba. Despite calling for social unity, Estrada's inclinations were more elitist; upon taking office, he supported the rights of U.S. capital over those of Cuban workers. Along with encouraging more foreign investment and large-scale agriculture (rather than a redistribution of land), he put former enemies of Cuban independence in high political posts. Even as he cultivated good relations with the United States (he had been a supporter of eventual annexation), he repressed his critics.[42] "This is not the Republic we fought for," commented General Máximo Gómez, former head of the Cuban revolutionary forces (Document 15).[43]

The military governor, General Leonard Wood, left Cuba on the day of Estrada's inauguration. But following the provisions of the Platt Amendment, the United States intervened again in 1906 to maintain "order" in the face of political strife. Further landings followed in 1912, 1917, and 1920. President Franklin Roosevelt repealed the Platt Amendment in 1934, in accordance with his Good Neighbor Policy, but the United States has retained the base at Guantánamo.[44]

PUERTO RICO

In July 1898, as part of the U.S. war effort against Spain, General Nelson A. Miles marched into Spain's Puerto Rican colony (known then to English-speakers as Porto Rico), promising the blessings of U.S. political principles. But instead of protecting, much less expanding, the political rights granted by Spain, the United States curtailed them. Rather than establishing a protectorate, as in the Cuban case, or granting Puerto Rico full independence, as Puerto Rican nationalists wanted, the United States annexed the island with the Foraker Act (also known as the Organic Act of 1900).[45]

The U.S. government set up a colonial structure modeled, in part, after the one set up by the British in the crown colony of Trinidad. It allowed islanders to elect a House of Delegates but gave the U.S. president the right to appoint a governor and top administrators. It also granted the U.S. Congress the right to annul Puerto Rican legislation that it found objectionable. Puerto Rico could send a delegate to the U.S. Congress, but this delegate could not vote. (Under Spanish rule, Puerto Rico had sent sixteen voting delegates to the Spanish parliament.) The Foraker Act undid the right to universal male suffrage and forbade Puerto Rico from making commercial treaties with other countries.[46]

Wealthy sugar and coffee producers eager for greater access to U.S. markets saw annexation as personally advantageous, as did some working people who had the opposite expectation—that U.S. rule would liberate them from elite oppression and usher in a great era for labor. Hopes for a social revolution were soon dashed. In addition to restricting suffrage to literate and taxpaying men, the United States decreed that only property holders could hold seats on municipal councils, and it coerced impoverished Puerto Ricans into plantation labor. Not having extended the Bill of Rights to Puerto Rico, U.S. officials prohibited criticism of the military government and U.S. policies. Afro–Puerto Ricans found themselves subject to assault by white U.S. soldiers who, despite all the talk of uplift, were deeply committed to racist hierarchies (Documents 5 and 35).[47]

The annexation of Puerto Rico brought the United States into murky constitutional waters. The Supreme Court tried to make sense of Puerto Rico's new status (as well as that of the nation's other new island acquisitions) in a series of decisions that came to be known as the Insular Cases. Decided by narrow one-vote margins, these cases became the legal backing for subsequent colonial policies. In *Downes v. Bidwell* (1901), the Court held that "the Island of Porto Rico is a territory appurtenant and belonging to the United States, but not a part of the United States within the revenue clauses of the Constitution" (Document 34).[48] A later case was brought by Isabel Gonzalez, who sailed from Puerto Rico to New York in August 1902. Widowed, pregnant, and nearly impoverished, she intended to join her brother and fiancé, who were working in factories on Staten Island. Immigration officials prevented the reunion. They detained her as "likely to become a public charge," a claim consistently applied to unmarried pregnant women. After failing to win admittance through proving her good character, Gonzalez broadened her argument: She claimed that she was not an alien because she hailed from Puerto Rico, a U.S. territory.[49]

The *Gonzales v. Williams* case anglicized the plaintiff's name as it spelled out a new legal category, which came to be known as a noncitizen U.S. national—a status between citizen and alien. This ruling countered the Reconstruction-era Fourteenth Amendment, which held that "all persons born or naturalized in the United States, and subject to the jurisdiction thereof, are citizens of the United States." As nationals, Gonzalez and other residents of U.S. territories were not subject to U.S. immigration restrictions. But they still did not qualify for U.S. citizenship until the passage of the Jones-Shafroth Act in 1917.[50] It was only in 1948 that Puerto Ricans won the right to elect their own governor. Puerto Rico became a U.S. commonwealth with limited self-rule in 1952. It retains that status to this day.[51]

HAWAI'I

After taking office in 1897, President McKinley sought to reverse his predecessor's policy toward Hawai'i by sending an annexation treaty to the Senate. One of the considerations that drove this decision was the threat posed by Japan, which had deployed several warships to the islands to protest anti-Japanese immigration practices. Given the size of the Japanese population on the islands, white planters feared that Hawai'i might someday become a Japanese colony if the United States did not annex it. Despite these concerns, the U.S. Senate did not muster the two-thirds majority necessary for ratification.

The war against Spain gave McKinley a second chance. Knowing that he still lacked the necessary sixty votes, he asked for a joint resolution of the House and Senate, which required only simple majorities. If earlier, Hawai'i's distance from U.S. shores had dampened annexationist ardor, events in the Philippine theater of the war against Spain made distance an asset. As a rising Pacific power, the United States would need naval bases and coaling stations. Hawai'i seemed a perfect place for both, at least to the U.S. congressmen who passed the joint resolution. The wider American empire continued to play a major role in Hawai'ian affairs, as seen, for example, in the transporting of more than five thousand Puerto Rican workers to Hawai'i to work on its sugar plantations between 1900 and 1901 (Document 39).[52]

INTERVENTION IN THE PHILIPPINES

Although the United States declared war against Spain due to the conflict in Cuba, the first battle of the war took place halfway around the world, in the Spanish colony of the Philippines, an archipelago of more than seven thousand islands with about 7.6 million inhabitants.[53] (See Map 2, enlarged area.) The explorer Ferdinand Magellan had claimed the islands for Spain in 1521, and they had long provided the cornerstone for Spanish trade in the Pacific. On May 1, 1898, Commodore (soon to be promoted to Admiral) George Dewey sank a Spanish flotilla in Manila Bay. It was a smashing victory: His squadron destroyed seven Spanish vessels with no loss of U.S. ships or lives. Initially, Dewey cooperated with the Filipino nationalists, led by Emilio Aguinaldo. Indeed, a U.S. steamer brought Aguinaldo back from exile in Hong Kong so that he could provide ground forces in the Philippines. But relations soon soured. Aguinaldo claimed that Dewey had promised independence to the Philippines; Dewey denied having done so.[54]

As in Cuba, the struggle for independence in the Philippines predated the U.S. intervention in 1898. One branch of the Filipino nationalist movement was led by wealthy European-educated Filipinos, known as *ilustrados*, among them, José Rizal, who formed a Philippine nationalist association in 1889. Rizal named the group Los Indios Bravos (the Indian

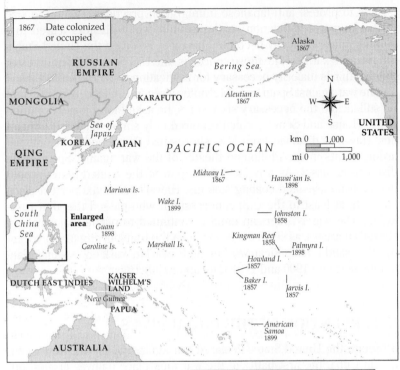

Map 2. *The U.S. Reach into the Pacific, ca. 1840–1914*

braves), in admiration of the Native American warriors he had seen in a Wild West show at the Paris Exposition.[55] Less wealthy Filipinos led by Andres Bonifacio formed another separatist secret society, called the Katipunan, in 1892. The Katipunan attempted to overthrow the Spanish in August 1898, but members lacked military expertise and firearms.[56]

As the Katipunan organized urban Filipinos in the Manila area, rural Filipinos increasingly protested the land and labor policies that benefitted Spanish friars and the elite families that leased land on the islands from the Catholic Church. By 1896, competing branches of the Katipunan were struggling for influence. Their efforts caused Spain to send reinforcements, at a time when it could ill afford to do so because of the resources it was expending in Cuba. In November 1897, revolutionary leaders passed a provisional constitution for a Filipino republic and selected the twenty-eight-year-old Aguinaldo as *presidente*.[57]

Not knowing how close the Spanish general Miguel Primo de Rivera was to conceding defeat, the Filipino revolutionaries accepted the offer of a truce in December 1897. Aguinaldo was among the Filipino revolutionaries who went into exile in the British colony of Hong Kong, following the conditions of the truce. But although the fighting let up, the revolution did not. The revolutionaries who had gathered in Hong Kong repudiated the truce on February 14, 1898, and rededicated themselves to purchasing arms. Dewey's destruction of the Spanish naval force in Manila Bay provided the opportunity to make their move. The exiled revolutionaries made their way back to the Philippines, determined to resume the revolution. Spanish efforts to ally with the Filipinos against the Americans came to naught as Filipino militia members turned their Spanish-issued rifles against Spanish forces. The revolution had spread so far beyond the secret circles of the Katipunan that Spanish defectors could be found in its ranks. In the aftermath of Dewey's victory, Filipino forces overran Spanish garrisons across the islands.[58]

Disregarding Aguinaldo's declaration of Filipino independence on June 12, 1898, the United States landed troops at Cavite on July 1. By then, the revolutionaries had laid siege to Manila, cutting off supplies to the Spanish and causing them to live on horse and buffalo meat. The Spanish forces were ready to surrender, but they followed the instructions from Madrid to capitulate to the Americans, not to the Filipinos. They did so following a mock battle on August 13, waged for the pride of the Spanish military, which did not want to return home in shame for having surrendered without a fight. The Filipino struggle for independence against Spain became an uneasy partnership with the United

States, a partnership so tense that U.S. and Filipino soldiers shoved each other on the streets.[59]

By December 1898, as the last of the Spanish troops departed the islands, revolutionary leaders were working to foster collaboration with the Muslim sultans who ruled the southern islands of the Philippines. The revolutionary government adopted a provisional constitution in Malolos in January 1899, thereby inaugurating a republic. On February 6, the U.S. Senate voted to ratify the Treaty of Paris, with just one vote beyond the constitutionally mandated two-thirds majority. The treaty resolved disputes between Spain and the United States, stipulating that Spain would cede the Philippines in exchange for $20 million. But the treaty did not settle matters in the Philippines, where fighting between U.S. and Filipino forces had begun two days earlier. Filipinos and Americans argued over who had fired the first shot, but the sum of the matter was that months of strained relationships had finally erupted into war, with each side convinced of its own right to sovereignty.[60]

CONDUCT OF THE WAR IN THE PHILIPPINES

Shortly after war broke out between the erstwhile allies, U.S. forces captured the Philippine Republic's capital at Malolos, about twenty-five miles from Manila. In the ensuing months, columns of U.S. soldiers would attack the Filipinos who were dug in along rice paddies and river crossings. The Filipino fighters would withdraw, and the U.S. column would then press on to the next entrenchment down the road. Though undefeated, the U.S. troops would turn back after a few days, plagued by fever, thirst, and heat exhaustion. Filipino soldiers would then rebuild their trenches and punish suspected collaborators.[61]

By 1900, the U.S. military and its Filipino collaborators had destroyed the Philippine army's capacity to wage a conventional war. Rather than surrender, Aguinaldo had his forces turn guerrilla. U.S. servicemen characterized Filipino resistance as "amigo warfare," by which they meant that Filipinos who were friends during the day became insurgents at night or whenever the opportunity arose. Frustrated by their inability to win via battlefield encounters, U.S. forces turned to the tactic that Americans had denounced in Cuba: concentrating civilians in camps to prevent them from aiding the *insurrectos*. American troops burned villages thought to be unfriendly. On occasion, U.S. soldiers extracted information through torture, including beatings and a technique known as the "water cure," which involved pumping water into a prostrate prisoner

(Document 22). The U.S. military also expanded the Philippine constabulary, staffed by Filipino men, whom they relied on for guides, intelligence, police for occupied areas, and supplements to U.S. troop strength. With the help of Filipino scouts, Colonel Frederick Funston captured Aguinaldo in March 1901. Following his capture, Aguinaldo urged cooperation with the Americans, but the fighting continued, spreading to the eastern island of Samar.[62]

In the fall of 1901, Filipino nationalists ambushed a Ninth Infantry company stationed in the small coastal town of Balangiga. Citing the roughly fifty U.S. deaths, the U.S. military called the episode a massacre, but their response led Filipinos to regard the massacre of Balangiga differently: The Americans retaliated by killing most of the inhabitants of the town (Document 21).[63] In the aftermath, General Jacob Smith reportedly told his subordinates to turn the interior of the island into a "howling wilderness." He authorized his troops to execute all males on the island over the age of ten and continued the policy of forcing the population into guarded concentration zones. "I want this war carried on with more severity," he told one of his captains. "In fact, it is more killing that I want."[64]

By the summer of 1902, the insurgent forces on Samar had been subdued to such an extent that President Theodore Roosevelt declared the war over. Having called it an "insurrection" at the start (a term that implies opposition to duly constituted authority), U.S. observers came to label further resistance mere "banditry."[65] Yet the fighting carried on, with so-called bandits raiding villages on the outskirts of Manila in 1904. A group known as Pulahanes took up the fight in the mountains of Samar, more for themselves than for a unified Philippine state. Whole villages joined the Pulahan campaign from 1904 to 1907.[66]

Muslim Filipinos, known as Moros, also continued to resist U.S. rule in the Moro Wars, which lasted from 1899 to 1912. The U.S. military denounced the Moros as slaveowners, pirates, polygamists, autocrats, feuders, and religious fanatics. But claims that the United States was a bearer of civilization lost credibility when U.S. Army forces machine-gunned resisters holed up in a volcanic crater at Bud Dajo, on the island of Jolo. Critics in the United States condemned the U.S. military for shooting women and children; the governor of the province, General Leonard Wood, responded by saying that the women and children had fought U.S. troops.[67]

Despite President McKinley's claims to benevolence, the Philippine war against the United States resulted in more Filipino deaths than three centuries of Spanish rule had.[68] The total number remains a subject of debate, in part due to the absence of census data for the prewar period and the unreliability of parish records of births and deaths. Early estimates lay in the 500,000 to 600,000 range. Later calculations reached as high as three million, though further assessments have questioned the accuracy of some of the numbers used in the calculations.[69] Even as the quest for a numerical accounting continues, it is clear that disease, hunger, and warfare took a heavy toll on the Philippine people.

The bloody struggle in the Philippines gave rise to a vocal anti-imperialist movement in the United States (Documents 28–32). Significantly, many so-called anti-imperialists did not object to U.S. expansion per se; they just had different ideas about where the United States should expand and who should be incorporated. In contrast to imperialists' assertions that people such as Filipinos needed paternalistic guidance, anti-imperialists insisted that the United States should not undermine its own democracy by annexing people incapable of self-government. Within these general patterns lie further variations in racial thinking. Imperialists disagreed over the possibilities for racial uplift (Documents 24, 26, and 27), and the anti-imperialist movement included African Americans and others who vehemently objected to white supremacist ideologies (Document 29).

GOVERNMENT IN THE PHILIPPINES

Although the Muslim islands in the southern Philippines remained under U.S. Army rule for over fourteen years, the United States began the transition to civilian rule in the northern Philippine islands even in the midst of the war.[70] In its efforts to establish a colonial government, the United States benefitted from Spain's previous colonization of the islands, for upon arrival U.S. officials found an educated, Westernized elite experienced in Spanish-style local rule. By 1901, U.S. forces had begun to set up municipal governments in provinces declared to be pacified. By 1907, it established the bicameral Philippine Assembly with veto power resting in the hands of U.S. authorities. Two political parties competed for power: the Partido Nacional Progresista, which called for eventual independence, and the Partido Nacionalista, which demanded immediate independence. Both parties urged U.S. officials to grant more government positions to Filipinos and more autonomy to local governments.[71]

By making suffrage dependent on property holdings and literacy as well as age (twenty-three or older) and gender (male), U.S. occupiers strengthened the power of the Philippine elite. The Philippine ruling class further extended its influence by serving as intermediaries between U.S. officials and the masses of the Philippine people.[72] As increasing numbers of the "better classes" collaborated with the U.S. authorities, peasants and workers continued to call for independence through armed rebellion. Constabulary agents infiltrated dissenting groups, resulting in the incarceration of organizers and the confiscation of weapons.[73]

The U.S. imperial state in the Philippines relied on local governments and public-private alliances—including with missionary groups—to achieve many of its policy goals. These goals were summed up by the term *benevolent assimilation*, which implied development along U.S. lines and integration into the U.S. economic system. A major priority was the establishment of English-language public schools. The occupation government also prioritized public health (Document 36). The United States distributed land via homestead legislation, improved roads and harbors, and established agricultural experiment stations. Revenues generated in the islands financed such programs.[74]

Given the relatively free hand they exercised, U.S. officials in the Philippines did not have to muster as much consent as politicians and administrators within the mainland United States. For example, the U.S. Army relied on a vast network of informers to gather information on the political elite, and it then used this information to keep the elite in line. Its methods, including photographic identification, influenced policing techniques in the United States.[75]

Colonial public health officials also exercised powers unprecedented in the United States. The Philippine Bureau of Health engaged in a massive social engineering project that involved changing toilet practices (through latrine construction and the use of lime to cover human waste), food handling, diets, and architecture. It quarantined suspected cholera carriers and conducted large-scale inoculation campaigns against smallpox. Some public health benefits followed from these policies, but there were also costs: neighborhoods burned to the ground, intensive bodily surveillance, the forced separation of "lepers" from their families and communities, and a tendency to stigmatize Filipinos as diseased (Document 37). Health officials' apparently beneficent intentions accompanied more self-serving ambitions: a more efficient workforce and a sounder environment for Americans who lacked immunities to local microbes.[76]

American officials tied the Philippine economy to the U.S. economy via more investment and a reduction in tariff barriers. By 1914, about half of Philippine exports went to the United States; by 1920, about 70 percent. The leading Philippine exports included sugar and tobacco. These tended to be grown by big planters, because smaller planters focused on rice. Access to the U.S. market thus increased the power of the landed oligarchy. Even as elite Filipinos publicly called for independence from the United States, some privately called for ongoing ties, so as to preserve the connections that benefitted them as a class.[77]

The 1912 election of Woodrow Wilson to the U.S. presidency brought a Democrat to the White House for the first time since the United States landed troops in the Philippines. Wilson pursued a policy of "Filipinization," which meant shifting power to Filipinos. Governor General Francis B. Harrison began to appoint Filipinos in large numbers to the civil service, so that by 1921, Filipinos held 90 percent of the government posts in the islands. The Jones Act of 1916 proclaimed the U.S. intention of withdrawing from the Philippines as soon as a stable government was established there, but it left the matter of determining readiness to the United States, which continued to defer independence. The 1934 Tydings-McDuffie Act finally set a date for Philippine independence: July 4, 1946. That promise was realized after a Japanese occupation in World War II and the U.S. reconquest of the islands from Japan.

BEYOND THE PHILIPPINES

The interventions of 1898—which extended to the Spanish colony of Guam (Document 33), as well as to Hawaii, Cuba, Puerto Rico, and the Philippines—provided precedents for further troop landings in East Asia and the Caribbean. In 1899, the United States claimed Wake Island, a Pacific atoll useful as a coal and cable station. Without consulting the Samoan people, it also annexed the eastern islands in the Samoan archipelago. In 1900, it joined with six European nations and Japan in landing troops in China during the Boxer Uprising.

President Theodore Roosevelt provided a rationale for additional interventions in his corollary to the Monroe Doctrine. Going well beyond Monroe's assertion that European powers should not intervene in the independent Latin American states, Roosevelt declared that the United States had a right to intervene if its interests were at stake. This attitude contributed to a score of early-twentieth-century interventions: the acquisition of the ten-mile-wide Panama Canal Zone in 1903; the placement of Panama as a whole under a protectorate the same year; the establishment of a customs receivership over the Dominican Republic in 1905 (Document 45); the stationing of Marines in Cuba under the conditions of the Platt Amendment in 1906, 1912, 1917, and 1920; the occupation of Veracruz, Mexico, in 1914 and a punitive expedition into Mexico in 1916–1917; the occupations of Nicaragua (1912–1925), Haiti (1915–1934) (Document 38), and the Dominican Republic (1916–1924); and the acquisition of the Danish Virgin Islands in 1917 (Document 7).[78] (See Map 3.)

The policies enacted in these various sites resembled each other in a number of ways, influenced as they were by European colonial practices, U.S. political precepts, and circulating personnel. Yet efforts to shape U.S. rule to local conditions also led to considerable variations from place to place. The lack of a central colonial office contributed to the variety in U.S. practice. The territories of New Mexico and Arizona became states in 1912.[79] Alaska and Hawaii fell under the aegis of the Interior Department. Puerto Rico, the Philippines, the Panama Canal Zone, the Dominican Republic occupation, and the Haitian occupation were administered through the War Department's Bureau of Insular Affairs. The Virgin Islands, Guam, and Samoa came under the control of the Navy Department. Native Americans in the contiguous United States were governed by the Bureau of Indian Affairs. These arrangements lasted until 1934, when President Franklin Roosevelt centralized territorial administration by establishing the Division of Territories and Island Possessions in the Interior Department.[80]

Despite its twentieth-century interventions, the United States did not expand the total amount of its territory. To the contrary, it reduced its sovereign reach by granting Cuba independence in 1902 and the Philippines independence in 1946. Despite the annexations of American Samoa, the Virgin Islands, the Northern Mariana Islands, the Panama Canal Zone (from 1903 to 1979), and the Pacific trust territories of the Marshall Islands and Palau (after World War II), the United States reached its maximum area between March 1899 and May 1902.[81] Rather than pursue further territorial enlargement, after 1898 the United States wielded power via short-term interventions, amenable national leaders, U.S.-trained national guards, economic leverage, the promotion of a capitalist world system, and its cultural sway, stemming from its positive image in many parts of the world.

EMPIRE AT HOME

All too often, U.S. history writings promote the conception of empire as something that happened "out there"—in other countries and offshore islands rather than in the continental United States. Such analyses overlook not only settler colonialism but also the role of empire as the engine of

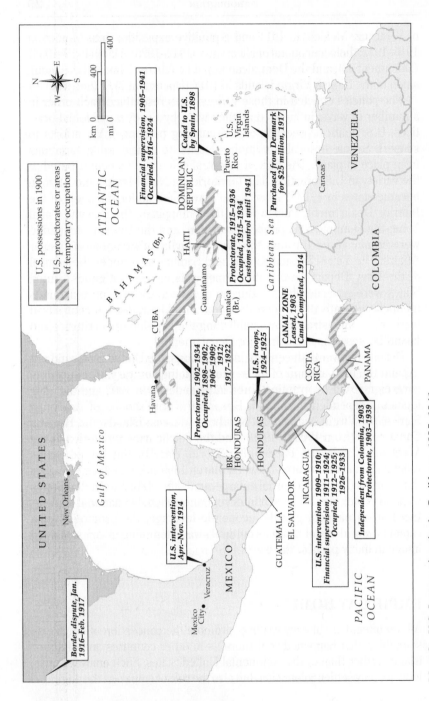

Map 3. *U.S. Interventions in the Caribbean, 1895–1941*

Legend:
- U.S. possessions in 1900
- U.S. protectorates or areas of temporary occupation

Border dispute, Jan. 1916–Feb. 1917

U.S. intervention, Apr.–Nov. 1914

Financial supervision, 1905–1941; Occupied, 1916–1924

Ceded to U.S. by Spain, 1898

Purchased from Denmark for $25 million, 1917

Protectorate, 1915–1936; Occupied, 1915–1934; Customs control until 1941

Protectorate, 1902–1934; Occupied, 1898–1902; 1906–1909; 1912; 1917–1922

U.S. troops, 1924–1925

CANAL ZONE Leased, 1903; Canal Completed, 1914

U.S. intervention, 1909–1910; Financial supervision, 1911–1924; Occupied, 1912–1925; 1926–1933

Independent from Colombia, 1903; Protectorate, 1903–1939

UNITED STATES

Gulf of Mexico

New Orleans

Mexico City · Veracruz

MEXICO

GUATEMALA

EL SALVADOR

BR. HONDURAS

HONDURAS

NICARAGUA

COSTA RICA

PANAMA

COLOMBIA

VENEZUELA

Caracas

PACIFIC OCEAN

ATLANTIC OCEAN

Caribbean Sea

B A H A M A S (Br.)

CUBA

Havana

Guantánamo

Jamaica (Br.)

HAITI

DOMINICAN REPUBLIC

Puerto Rico

U.S. Virgin Islands

km 0   400
mi 0   400

26

globalization before World War II. Imperial connections drew the United States as deeply into global currents as the polities under its control. In addition to their effects on the U.S. economy, imperial endeavors profoundly affected U.S. culture. As imperial transportation networks opened up wider sources of supply, U.S. consumers literally bought into empire, and not just that of their own nation, as seen in advertisements for goods such as curry powders, Oriental carpets, silks, and tea (Documents 47 and 48).[82] World's fairs, amusement parks, museums, missionary fund-raisers, and traveling picture shows also played major roles in infusing the stuff of empire into U.S. daily life (Document 2). Children played board games on the Cuban War; circuses depicted Hindu people performing supposed "Hindoo" ceremonies; department store windows contained ersatz Guatemalan villages. Buffalo Bill's Wild West show featured attacks on settlers' cabins and reenactments of "Custer's Last Rally"; by the turn of the twentieth century, it included San Juan Hill reenactments and other thrilling spectacles based loosely on the Philippine-American War, the Boxer intervention, and other imperial conflicts. From advertisements to household decorations, recipes, travel writings, textbooks, fiction, tourist itineraries, and films, U.S. culture revealed engagement with empire.[83]

One of the most momentous domestic legacies for imperial interventions by the United States has been the resulting changes in the American people. Prior to World War II, over 12 percent of the people governed by the United States lived in its overseas colonies. Not only did the United States come to encompass new island-dwelling populations, but its interventions also sparked new migration streams. Millions of Mexicans came to the U.S. Southwest between 1900 and 1930; Puerto Ricans started migrating to the mainland United States in significant numbers in the 1950s; Cubans and Dominicans followed in the 1960s. As Yen Le Espiritu remarked in a book on Filipino Americans, "Filipinos went to the United States because Americans went first to the Philippines. In other words, Filipino migration to the United States must be understood within the context of U.S. imperialism in the Philippines and in Asia."[84]

THE IMPERIAL ORIGINS OF OUR OWN GLOBAL AGE

To understand our own contemporary global moment, we need to look back to this earlier age of globalization and the ways that it was shaped by imperial connections and conflicts. This deeper historical perspective can help us understand the power relations that gave rise to the world system we inhabit today. It reveals how the search for national security and wealth has, in many instances, generated insecurities and hardships for others. It teaches us that the United States has never been able to unilaterally impose its will on the world; that even colonized peoples disparaged by U.S. policymakers have shaped the contours of U.S. foreign relations and the nature of U.S. imperial power. Glancing back to the years around 1898 also shows how cultural assumptions such as ideas about race and religion have shaped relations once thought to be driven by rational calculations of national interest (Documents 40–43). Just as significantly, attention to empire makes it clear that American democracy has been developed and contested on a geographic scale spilling well beyond the bounds of the fifty current states. Acknowledging the importance of empire to U.S. history can help us appreciate the nation's place in a larger global context and the world's place in the history of the nation.

NOTES

[1]James Belich, *Replenishing the Earth: The Settler Revolution and the Rise of the Anglo-World, 1783–1939* (Oxford: Oxford University Press, 2009).

[2]Pekka Hämäläinen, *The Comanche Empire* (New Haven, Conn.: Yale University Press, 2008); John Darwin, *Unfinished Empire: The Global Expansion of Britain* (London: Allen Lane, 2012), 11–12, 305, 394; Bouda Etemad, *Possessing the World: Taking the Measurements of Colonisation from the Eighteenth to the Twentieth Century*, translated from the French by Andrene Everson (New York: Berghahn Books, 2007), 165–67.

[3]Emily S. Rosenberg, ed., *A World Connecting: 1870–1945* (Cambridge, Mass.: Belknap Press of Harvard University Press, 2012); E. J. Hobsbawm, *The Age of Empire, 1875–1914* (New York: Pantheon Books, 1987), 15, 57–58.

[4]Jay Sexton, *The Monroe Doctrine: Empire and Nation in Nineteenth-Century America* (New York: Hill and Wang, 2011), 7; Emily Rosenberg, *Spreading the American Dream* (Boston: Hill and Wang, 1982), 131; Erez Manela, *The Wilsonian Moment: Self-Determination and the International Origins of Anticolonial Nationalism* (New York: Oxford University Press, 2007).

[5]Brian DeLay, "Indian Polities, Empire, and the History of American Foreign Relations," *Diplomatic History* 39 (November 2015): 927–42.

[6]Michael Adas, "From Settler Colony to Global Hegemon: Integrating the Exceptionalist Narrative of the American Experience into World History," *American Historical Review* 106 (December 2001): 1692–720; Amy S. Greenberg, *A Wicked War: Polk, Clay, Lincoln, and the 1846 U.S. Invasion of Mexico* (New York: Alfred A. Knopf, 2012), 259; Brian DeLay, *War of a Thousand Deserts: Indian Raids and the U.S.-Mexican War* (New Haven, Conn.: Yale University Press, 2008).

[7]Jeffrey Ostler, *The Plains Sioux and U.S. Colonialism from Lewis and Clark to Wounded Knee* (New York: Cambridge University Press, 2004).

[8]Claude A. Clegg III, *The Price of Liberty: African Americans and the Making of Liberia* (Chapel Hill: University of North Carolina Press, 2004); Brandon Mills, "'The United States of Africa': Liberian Independence and the Contested Meaning of a Black Republic," *Journal of the Early Republic* 34 (Spring 2014): 79–107.

[9]Greg Grandin, *The Empire of Necessity: Slavery, Freedom, and Deception in the New World* (New York: Metropolitan Books, 2014); Ian Tyrrell, *Reforming the World: The Creation of America's Moral Empire* (Princeton, N.J.: Princeton University Press, 2010); Matthew Pratt Guterl, *American Mediterranean: Southern Slaveholders in the Age of Emancipation*

(Cambridge, Mass.: Harvard University Press, 2008); Aims McGuinness, *Path of Empire: Panama and the California Gold Rush* (Ithaca, N.Y.: Cornell University Press, 2008); Amy S. Greenberg, *Manifest Manhood and the Antebellum American Empire* (New York: Cambridge University Press, 2005).

[10] Gordon H. Chang, "Whose 'Barbarism'? Whose 'Treachery'? Race and Civilization in the Unknown United States–Korea War of 1871," *Journal of American History* 89 (March 2003): 1331–65.

[11] Teemu Ruskola, "Canton Is Not Boston: The Invention of American Imperial Sovereignty," *American Quarterly* 57 (September 2005): 859–84.

[12] Ian Tyrrell, *Transnational Nation: United States History in Global Perspective since 1789* (New York: Palgrave Macmillan, 2007), 89; Jimmy M. Skaggs, *The Great Guano Rush: Entrepreneurs and American Overseas Expansion* (New York: St. Martin's Press, 1994); Eric Love, *Race over Empire: Racism and U.S. Imperialism, 1865–1900* (Chapel Hill: University of North Carolina Press, 2004), 27–72.

[13] Brian McAllister Linn, *The Philippine War, 1899–1902* (Lawrence: University Press of Kansas, 2000), 8; Nina Silber, *The Romance of Reunion: Northerners and the South, 1865–1900* (Chapel Hill: University of North Carolina Press, 1993).

[14] Paul A. Kramer, "Empires, Exceptions and Anglo-Saxons: Race and Rule between the British and United States Empires, 1880–1910," *Journal of American History* 88 (March 2002): 1315–53.

[15] Walter LaFeber, *The American Search for Opportunity, 1865–1913*, Cambridge History of American Foreign Relations, vol. 2 (Cambridge: Cambridge University Press, 1993), 46–52.

[16] Ibid., 165.

[17] John Mason Hart, *Empire and Revolution: The Americans in Mexico since the Civil War* (Berkeley: University of California Press, 2002), 71–200, 260.

[18] Mira Wilkins, *The Emergence of Multinational Enterprise: American Business Abroad from the Colonial Era to 1914* (Cambridge, Mass.: Harvard University Press, 1970), 36, 65, 81–83, 113, 134, 151.

[19] Barry Rigby, "The Origins of American Expansion in Hawaii and Samoa, 1865–1900," *International History Review* 10 (May 1988): 221–37, 232.

[20] Robert L. Beisner, *From the Old Diplomacy to the New, 1865–1900*, 2nd ed. (1975; Wheeling, Ill.: Harland Davidson, 1986).

[21] Tyrrell, *Reforming the World*; LaFeber, *The American Search for Opportunity*, 99–100.

[22] Michael H. Hunt, *The Making of a Special Relationship: The United States and China to 1914* (New York: Columbia University Press, 1983), 162, 186.

[23] Sally Engle Merry, *Colonizing Hawai'i: The Cultural Power of Law* (Princeton, N.J.: Princeton University Press, 2000), 35.

[24] Ada Ferrer, *Insurgent Cuba: Race, Nation, and Revolution, 1868–1898* (Chapel Hill: University of North Carolina Press, 1999), 2, 95; Rebecca J. Scott, *Slave Emancipation in Cuba: The Transition to Free Labor, 1860–1899* (Pittsburgh: University of Pittsburgh Press, 1985), 288; Aline Helg, *Our Rightful Share: The Afro-Cuban Struggle for Equality, 1886–1912* (Chapel Hill: University of North Carolina Press, 1995), 3.

[25] Louis A. Pérez Jr., *On Becoming Cuban: Identity, Nationality, and Culture* (1999; Chapel Hill: University of North Carolina Press, 2008), 28–29, 37, 44.

[26] Walter LaFeber, *The American Age: United States Foreign Policy at Home and Abroad since 1750* (New York: W. W. Norton, 1989), 185.

[27] John Lawrence Tone, *War and Genocide in Cuba, 1895–1898* (Chapel Hill: University of North Carolina Press, 2006), 9–10, 59–60, 108, 193.

[28] Kristin L. Hoganson, *Fighting for American Manhood: How Gender Politics Provoked the Spanish-American and Philippine-American Wars* (New Haven, Conn.: Yale University Press, 1998), 68–106, 240–42.

[29] Louis A. Pérez, *Cuba between Empires, 1898–1902* (Pittsburgh: University of Pittsburgh Press, 1983), 65.

[30] David M. Pletcher, "1861–1898: Economic Growth and Diplomatic Adjustment," in *Economics and World Power: An Assessment of American Diplomacy since 1789*, ed. William H.

Becker and Samuel F. Wells Jr. (New York: Columbia University Press, 1984), 119–71, 166.

[31] Bonnie M. Miller, *From Liberation to Conquest: The Visual and Popular Cultures of the Spanish-American War of 1898* (Amherst: University of Massachusetts Press, 2011), 11.

[32] Louis A. Pérez Jr., *The War of 1898: The United States and Cuba in History and Historiography* (Chapel Hill: University of North Carolina Press, 1998).

[33] Helg, *Our Rightful Share*, 94–97.

[34] Hoganson, *Fighting for American Manhood*, 39.

[35] Kenneth E. Hendrickson Jr., *The Spanish-American War* (Westport, Conn.: Greenwood Press, 2003), 10.

[36] Harold Sprout and Margaret Sprout, *The Rise of American Naval Power, 1776–1918*, 5th ed. (1939; Annapolis, Md.: Naval Institute Press, 1980), 233–37.

[37] Hendrickson, *The Spanish-American War*, 32–33; Pérez, *The War of 1898*, 21–22.

[38] Thomas Schoonover, *Uncle Sam's War of 1898 and the Origins of Globalization* (Lexington: University Press of Kentucky, 2003), 83.

[39] Pérez, *The War of 1898*, 89–94; Hoganson, *Fighting for American Manhood*, 25–26.

[40] Lester D. Langley, *The United States and the Caribbean in the Twentieth Century* (1980; Athens: University of Georgia Press, 1982), 19; Helg, *Our Rightful Share*, 94–97.

[41] Pérez, *The War of 1898*, 33–34.

[42] Lillian Guerra, *The Myth of José Martí: Conflicting Nationalisms in Early Twentieth-Century Cuba* (Chapel Hill: University of North Carolina Press, 2005), 2, 15, 121–28.

[43] Gómez, cited in Pérez, *Cuba between Empires*, xv.

[44] Langley, *The United States and the Caribbean in the Twentieth Century*, 39–41.

[45] José Trías Monge, *Puerto Rico: The Trials of the Oldest Colony in the World* (New Haven, Conn.: Yale University Press, 1997), 42.

[46] Ibid., 43.

[47] Eileen J. Suárez Findlay, *Imposing Decency: The Politics of Sexuality and Race in Puerto Rico, 1870–1920* (Durham, N.C.: Duke University Press, 1999), chap. 4; on the bill of rights, Lanny Thompson, "The Imperial Republic: A Comparison of the Insular Territories under U.S. Dominion after 1898," *Pacific Historical Review* 71 (November 2002): 535–74, 559.

[48] Bartholomew H. Sparrow, *The Insular Cases and the Emergence of American Empire* (Lawrence: University Press of Kansas, 2006), 90.

[49] Sam Erman, "Meanings of Citizenship in the U.S. Empire: Puerto Rico, Isabel Gonzalez, and the Supreme Court, 1898 to 1905," *Journal of American Ethnic History* 27 (Summer 2008): 5–33, 15.

[50] Robert C. McGreevey, "Empire and Migration: Coastwise Shipping, National Status, and the Colonial Legal Origins of Puerto Rican Migration to the United States," *The Journal of the Gilded Age and Progressive Era* 11 (October 2012): 553–73, 553–54; Christina Duffy Burnett, "Empire and the Transformation of Citizenship," in *Colonial Crucible: Empire in the Making of the Modern American State*, ed. Alfred W. McCoy and Francisco A. Scarano (Madison: University of Wisconsin Press, 2009), 332–41.

[51] Juan Gonzalez, *Harvest of Empire: A History of Latinos in America* (New York: Viking Press, 2000), 61–62.

[52] Ibid., 62.

[53] Linn, *The Philippine War*, 15.

[54] David J. Silbey, *A War of Frontier and Empire: The Philippine-American War, 1899–1902* (New York: Hill and Wang, 2007), 6–7, 39–41.

[55] Ibid., 12.

[56] John N. Schumacher, *The Propaganda Movement, 1880–1895: The Creation of a Filipino Consciousness, the Making of a Revolution*, rev. ed. (Manila: Ateneo de Manila University Press, 1997), 33–83, 293; Reynaldo Clemeña Ileto, *Pasyon and Revolution: Popular Movements in the Philippines, 1840–1910* (Quezon City: Ateneo de Manila University Press, 1979), 4, 98.

[57] Onofre D. Corpuz, "The Filipino Revolution in Our Collective Memory," in *The Philippine Revolution and Beyond*, vol. 1, ed. Elmer A. Ordoñez (Manila: Philippine Centennial Commission, 1998), 3–42, 7–14.

[58] Ibid., 7, 15–19, 23–24, 28.

[59] Linn, *The Philippine War*, 37.

[60] Corpuz, "The Filipino Revolution in Our Collective Memory," 19, 32–35.

[61] Brian McAllister Linn, *Guardians of Empire: The U.S. Army and the Pacific, 1902–1940* (Chapel Hill: University of North Carolina Press, 1997), 11; Linn, *The Philippine War*, 185.

[62] Reynaldo C. Ileto, "The Philippine-American War: Friendship and Forgetting," in *Vestiges of War: The Philippine-American War and the Aftermath of an Imperial Dream, 1899–1999*, ed. Angel Velasco Shaw and Luis H. Francia (New York: New York University Press, 2002), 3–21, 4–7; Linn, *Guardians of Empire*, 12; Silbey, *A War of Frontier and Empire*, 164–68, 177, 179.

[63] Sharon Delmendo, *The Star-Entangled Banner: One Hundred Years of America in the Philippines* (New Brunswick, N.J.: Rutgers University Press, 2004), 170.

[64] Smith, cited in Linn, *The Philippine War*, 314–15.

[65] Ileto, "The Philippine-American War," 4–5.

[66] Linn, *Guardians of Empire*, 28, 31.

[67] Corpuz, "The Filipino Revolution in Our Collective Memory," 4; Linn, *Guardians of Empire*, 39.

[68] Schoonover, *Uncle Sam's War of 1898 and the Origins of Globalization*, 95.

[69] John M. Gates, "War-Related Deaths in the Philippines, 1898–1902," *Pacific Historical Review* 53 (August 1984): 367–78.

[70] Patricio N. Abinales, "The U.S. Army as an Occupying Force in Muslim Mindanao, 1899–1913," in *Colonial Crucible: Empire in the Making of the Modern American State*, ed. Alfred W. McCoy and Francisco A. Scarano (Madison: University of Wisconsin Press, 2009), 410–20, 410.

[71] Glenn Anthony May, *Social Engineering in the Philippines: The Aims, Execution, and Impact of American Colonial Policy, 1900–1913* (Westport, Conn.: Greenwood Press, 1980), xvi, 59–60; Brian McAllister Linn, *The U.S. Army and Counterinsurgency in the Philippine War, 1899–1902* (Chapel Hill: University of North Carolina Press, 1989), 26.

[72] May, *Social Engineering in the Philippines*, 42, 45; Peter W. Stanley, "Introduction," in *Reappraising an Empire: New Perspectives on Philippine-American History*, ed. Peter W. Stanley (Cambridge, Mass.: Harvard University Press, 1984), 1–10, 5.

[73] Reynaldo C. Ileto, *Filipinos and Their Revolution: Event, Discourse and Historiography* (Manila: Ateneo de Manila University Press, 1998), 89, 137–63.

[74] Alfred W. McCoy, Francisco A. Scarano, and Courtney Johnson, "On the Tropic of Cancer: Transitions and Transformations in the U.S. Imperial State," in *Colonial Crucible: Empire in the Making of the Modern American State*, ed. Alfred W. McCoy and Francisco A. Scarano (Madison: University of Wisconsin Press, 2009), 7; May, *Social Engineering in the Philippines*, 139, 146, 180.

[75] Alfred W. McCoy, "Policing the Imperial Periphery," in *Colonial Crucible: Empire in the Making of the Modern American State*, ed. Alfred W. McCoy and Francisco A. Scarano (Madison: University of Wisconsin Press, 2009), 106–15.

[76] Warwick Anderson, *Colonial Pathologies: American Tropical Medicine, Race, and Hygiene in the Philippines* (Durham, N.C.: Duke University Press, 2006), 8, 65, 95, 128, 159, 189, 233.

[77] May, *Social Engineering in the Philippines*, 139, 160, 181.

[78] Benjamin R. Beede, ed., *The War of 1898 and U.S. Interventions, 1898–1934: An Encyclopedia* (New York: Garland, 1994).

[79] Pablo Mitchell, *Coyote Nation: Sexuality, Race, and Conquest in Modernizing New Mexico, 1880–1920* (Chicago: University of Chicago Press, 2005), 17, 179.

[80] Julian Go, *Patterns of Empire: The British and American Empires, 1688 to the Present* (New York: Cambridge University Press, 2011), 62, 93.

[81] Sparrow, *The Insular Cases and the Emergence of American Empire*, 216.

[82] Kristin L. Hoganson, *Consumers' Imperium: The Global Production of American Domesticity, 1865–1920* (Chapel Hill: University of North Carolina Press, 2007).

[83] "The Parker Games," ad in *The Century Magazine* 57 (November 1898): n.p.; Robert W. Rydell, *All the World's a Fair* (Chicago: University of Chicago Press, 1984); Janet M. Davis, *The Circus Age: Culture and Society under the American Big Top* (Chapel Hill: University of North Carolina Press, 2002), 215–19; Hoganson, *Consumer's Imperium*, 179; Louis S. Warren, *Buffalo Bill's America: William Cody and the Wild West Show* (New York: Alfred A. Knopf, 2005), 31, 268, 428, 465–66.

[84] Daniel Immerwahr, "The Greater United States: Territory and Empire in U.S. History," *Diplomatic History*, advanced access version, May 6, 2016, doi10.1093/dh/dhw009; Yen Le Espiritu, *Home Bound: Filipino American Lives across Cultures, Communities, and Countries* (Berkeley: University of California Press, 2003), 25; Jesse Hoffnung-Garskof, "The Immigration Reform Act of 1965," in *The Familiar Made Strange: American Icons and Artifacts after the Transnational Turn*, ed. Brooke Blower and Mark Philip Bradley (Ithaca, N.Y.: Cornell University Press, 2015), 125–40.

PART TWO

The Documents

1

The United States in an Age of Empire

1

FREDERICK DOUGLASS

What Do We Want of San Domingo?

1871

Frederick Douglass, who had become a leading abolitionist following his escape from slavery, delivered these remarks on the annexation of Santo Domingo (the Dominican Republic) at a time when Reconstruction politics made him optimistic about the possibility of racial equality in the United States. But Douglass would not always support his fellow Republicans' expansionist visions, especially after white supremacists began to roll back democratic rights at the end of Reconstruction. In 1891, Douglass resigned from his diplomatic post as U.S. minister to Haiti to protest U.S. efforts to obtain a coaling station there against the will of the Haitian government.

A large audience assembled last evening at the Union Park Congregational Church, to hear Fred. Douglass speak of Santo Domingo. . . . Mr. Douglass closed his lecture by giving the reasons for the annexation of Santo Domingo to the United States:

1. The Latin civilization, whatever may have been its merits and achievements in other times and places, here in Santo Domingo has been a most conspicuous and wretched failure. It has, after three centuries' experience, conducted one of the most

"Santo Domingo," *Chicago Tribune*, December 30, 1871.

beautiful and productive countries in the world to the verge of depopulation.

2. Although the climate of Santo Domingo makes protracted physical effort uninviting, by invention and by wise division of the hours of labor, sufficient work can be done there to make the conditions of the laboring man as comfortable and happy as anywhere in this world.

3. The decay and ruin of this island is to be explained by the fact that the nations which have owned it hitherto have never had the good of its people at heart, and never made their improvement and happiness an object of their legislation. With them it was not the flock but the fleece.

4. While a large proportion of the present population are peaceable, owing to the ignorance entailed upon them by slavery and bad government, they are easily excited, and thrown into revolutionary movements wholly unfavorable to industry, and to the acquisition of wealth. They are at the mercy of designing chiefs, who keep the country in a constant turmoil.

5. Society has been running so long in the deeply worn grooves of this order, and has become so exhausted thereby, that there does not seem to be sufficient strength and vitality to lift itself out of those grooves.

6. This view of the situation is taken by the most intelligent and patriotic men with whom the speaker conversed while on the island.

7. A large majority of the people of the island believe their only salvation is in placing themselves under a strong government. By this means they think themselves able to put an end to revolution, by making successful revolution impossible.

8. A large majority of the people of Santo Domingo are in favor of the annexation of their country to the United States. For himself, the speaker said he thought the measure would be a good thing for Santo Domingo, and not a bad thing for the United States.... He replied to several objections, such as, "What do we want of San Domingo?" ... What do we want with anything on earth at all? What does England want of Jamaica, or of any other of her West India possessions? We are the only great power in the world not represented by some territorial possession in the West Indies.

The speaker referred to the statement that society in the tropics had never succeeded except under a despotic power, and said that the experiment had never been fairly tried. It would be time enough to adopt that theory when the Saxon race had tried its hand. If the Latins had not succeeded, that was no reason why the Saxon race could not succeed.

2

FREDERICK BURR OPPER

Uncle Sam's Show

1893

In 1893, Chicago hosted a world's fair known as the Columbian Exposition. Following the model of European fairs, it drew attention to the supposed contrasts between civilization and savagery in its official exhibits and in the adjacent commercial entertainment strip known as the Midway. This illustration alludes to some of the peoples represented at the fair (from left to right): Chinese, Spanish, Russian, English, U.S., German, French, Italian, and Dahomean.

VICTOR GILLAM

The White Man's Burden

1899

---

*This illustration references a poem published in February 1899 by British
author Rudyard Kipling. Titled "The White Man's Burden: The United
States and the Philippine Islands," the poem begins as follows: "Take up
the White Man's burden—/ Send forth the best ye breed—/ Go send your
sons to exile / To serve your captives' need / To wait in heavy harness /
On fluttered folk and wild—/ Your new-caught, sullen peoples, / Half
devil and half child." This cartoon was just one of many responses to the
poem. In April 1899,* The Colored American *published a parody including these lines: "To h— with the 'White Man's Burden!' / To h— with
Kipling's verse! / The Black Man demands our attention: / His condition
is growing worse."*

Victor Gillam, *Judge* (April 1, 1899).

"THE WHITE MAN'S BURDEN."

4

JOHN ELFRETH WATKINS JR.

We Have Much to Learn in Africa Today
1899

This document pertains to the Boer War (1899–1902), fought between the British and Dutch settlers (called Boers, from the Dutch word for "farmer") over the South African lands of Transvaal and the Orange Free State. Though successful in the end, the British found the struggle far more costly than they had expected. Boers and black Africans—many forced into concentration camps so they could not supply anti-British guerrillas—found the war more devastating still. Although there was widespread public sympathy in the United States for the underdog Boers, the United States declared neutrality and, in practice, leaned toward the British side, thereby fostering warmer ties with Britain in the years leading up to World War I. The author of this document, John Elfreth Watkins Jr., published widely on mechanical and military topics.

The Boer trouble has added extra zeal to Uncle Sam's present interest in African problems from which he expects to learn some lessons valuable in his task of successfully colonizing the Philippines. To take a selfish view, a war involving the newly subjected regions of the Dark Continent and thus attracting American military attaches and war correspondents to these wilds, where we have no official representatives, would be to our benefit. Portable huts, such as are being introduced into South Africa this year, would doubtless be of great value to us in teaching Philippine natives elementary principles of enlightened housekeeping. These domiciles, shipped from Glasgow, are made in detachable pieces such as can be put together by the most unskilled and in a surprisingly short time. They are constructed of "mild" steel with pine floors, sides of sheeting jointed with tubes, windows, combined shutters and sunshades and pine doors. The roofs are of jointed, double-sheeted panels, the space between the sheets being packed with non-conducting

John Elfreth Watkins Jr., "American Interests: How They Will Be Cared for in the South African War," *Los Angeles Times*, October 29, 1899.

material as a protection from heat. The diameter of such a home, in place, is 10 feet, the height 7 feet. Folding iron bedsteads, folding chairs, folding tables of iron and wood and portable stoves with ash-trays and chimneys are also supplied. In changing his neighborhood the house-holder simply disjoints his home and carries it away in two easily trans-ported boxes.

We might profit furthermore from a study of England's experiences in encouraging agriculture and stock breeding in her African posses-sions. In Rhodesia herds of Angora goats and Merino sheep are being introduced. Wagon roads are being rapidly opened and their extent is already nearly three thousand miles. Mining is being rapidly encour-aged in this protectorate by application of particularly liberal mining laws, under which a prospector is neither restricted to a single claim nor required to pay any tax or royalty until his mine is developed. Fur-ther encouragement to hasten development is a new system by which prospectors are supplied gratis with engineers for examining promising claims and are advanced a part of their working capital. In British Cen-tral Africa good roads are being constructed in all directions and several thousand acres are being cleared for coffee plantations, rice and wheat. Sheep and other live stock are being introduced, and the woolen indus-try is being encouraged. On the coast of British East Africa the English already have a flourishing little city, Mombasa, with 25,000 population, a submarine cable and a 600-mile railway now half completed to Victoria Nyanza, a lake about the size of Lake Superior. In Uganda, adjacent to this great lake and only a few years ago one of the wildest spots in Africa, English colonization has gone so far as the recent establishment of crimi-nal courts and a native parliament. Although an infant son of the black King Mwanga nominally reigns above this legislative body, the real exec-utive of the protectorate is the British commissioner. The object of the arrangement is to humor the natives much as we are doing in the Sultan-ate of Sulu.[1] . . .

Not alone from England, but also from conservative Germany might we gather in Africa some valuable hints as to the colonization of the Phil-ippines. In German Africa palms, coffee bushes, tobacco, cocoa, cloves and other valuable tropical plants are being widely introduced through scattered experiment stations and gardens. In French Africa Uncle Sam will find a combination comparable to what he has in the Philippines—Mohammedans and Negritos. Among the former element—Moors and

---

[1]A Muslim state in the southwestern part of the Philippine archipelago, initially governed by the United States through its existing elite.

Berbers—progress of civilization is slow, while among the negritic tribes the suppression of slave-raiding and cannibalism has occupied the chief attention of the French, up to the present time. In French Congo the tribes are genuine savages, always at war with one another, and often cannibals. They are available only as carriers and paddlers, being incapable of performing regular labor. In the African colonies of the other two great Latin powers, Italy and Spain, little development has taken place. Here is but another instance of the advance of the Anglo-Saxon over the Latin.

5

ISABEL GONZALEZ

Let Them Learn a Lesson from Great Britain
1905

Isabel Gonzalez was the plaintiff in the Gonzales v. Williams *case that established the legal category of the noncitizen U.S. national. The Court anglicized the spelling of her name. Although she had qualified for U.S. citizenship by virtue of marriage by the time the case made it to the Supreme Court, she kept her marriage secret in hopes of establishing U.S. citizenship for all Puerto Ricans. The following letter is one of several she wrote that were published in the* New York Times *after the* Gonzales *decision. Since Gonzalez does not speak for herself in the trial records, it is through her letters that we can glimpse her views on U.S. policy toward Puerto Rico and its relation to other colonial practices.*

The steady policy of the present Administration has been the compulsion of the natives to unlearn the methods acquired through four centuries of Iberian domination. It has paid more attention to make them discard, violently, the customs of their ancient rulers than to have them learn the modern systems and practices that would render easier the

Isabel Gonzalez, "Where England Shows Tact: It Is in Respecting Local Laws and Customs in Her Colonies," *New York Times*, September 3, 1905.

task of preparation for the life, liberty, and the pursuit of happiness. . . . The eagerness of the Americans to constrain them to give up cock-fighting, their relaxed Sabbath, bullfighting, &c., plainly shows that they went at it not with any evangelistic desire to impart to the natives the advantages for their enlightenment.

Let them learn a lesson from Great Britain, and note how she relies for the success of her colonial policy upon scrupulous respect for the local laws and customs of her varied possessions. The Hindoo or the Mogul who goes to law to-day may appeal for justice to the Royal Tribunal of London, and law cases are settled in accordance with the codes of those lands, that is to say, the Purana[1] and the Koran. In the Ionic Islands the Justinian Code is in force at present, conjointly with the decisions of the Admiralty Tribunal. In Canada the ordinances of the Kings of France can be discerned in her autonomic laws. In the Isle of France the Code of Napoleon rules, in the Anglo-Spanish Antilles it is the Laws of Castile and Aragon, while Dutch law governs the Cape of Good Hope.

Porto Rico's organic laws are clogged with different States' codes, imposed on her by the American rulers who have carried to the island the system of laws corresponding to the places from which they hailed and for which they felt most inclined. The lack of uniformity has been carried to such an extent that, in order to gain a good reputation as a lawyer in the Porto Rican bar, a man has to be both a Solomon and a Sandow.[2] I say a Sandow, because the lawyer will find it necessary to carry along with him so many books of consultation that the strength of that athlete would be very useful for the terrible task.

---

[1] Ancient Hindu texts.
[2] Eugen Sandow (1867–1925), a celebrity bodybuilder of the time.

6

W. E. BURGHARDT DU BOIS

Ownership of Materials and Men in the Darker World

1915

An early leader of the National Association for the Advancement of Colored People and one of the most notable U.S. intellectuals of his era, William Edward Burghardt Du Bois is perhaps best known for Souls of Black Folk *(1902), which argued that "the problem of the twentieth century is the problem of the color-line, — the relation of the darker to the lighter races of men in Asia and Africa, in America and the islands of the sea." In this essay, written during World War I, Du Bois grapples with the seeming paradox of broadening democratic commitments within Europe in a time of expanding imperial rule over non-European peoples.*

With the waning of the possibility of the Big Fortune, gathered by starvation wage and boundless exploitation of one's weaker and poorer fellows at home, arose more magnificently the dream of exploitation abroad. Always, of course, the individual merchant had at his own risk and in his own way tapped the riches of foreign lands. Later, special trading monopolies had entered the field and founded empires over-seas. Soon, however, the mass of merchants at home demanded a share in this golden stream; and finally, in the twentieth century, the laborer at home is demanding and beginning to receive a part of his share.

The theory of this new democratic despotism has not been clearly formulated. Most philosophers see the ship of state launched on the broad, irresistible tide of democracy, with only delaying eddies here and there; others, looking closer, are more disturbed. Are we, they ask, reverting to aristocracy and despotism—the rule of might? They cry out and then rub their eyes, for surely they cannot fail to see strengthening democracy all about them?

W. E. Burghardt Du Bois, "The African Roots of War," *Atlantic Monthly* 115 (May 1915): 709–12.

It is this paradox which has confounded philanthropists, curiously betrayed the Socialists, and reconciled the Imperialists and captains of industry to any amount of "Democracy." It is this paradox which allows in America the most rapid advance of democracy to go hand in hand in its very centres with increased aristocracy and hatred toward darker races, and which excuses and defends an inhumanity that does not shrink from the public burning of human beings.

Yet the paradox is easily explained: the white workingman has been asked to share the spoil of exploiting "chinks and niggers." It is no longer simply the merchant prince, or the aristocratic monopoly, or even the employing class, that is exploiting the world: it is the nation; a new democratic nation composed of united capital and labor. The laborers are not yet getting, to be sure, as large a share as they want or will get, and there are still at the bottom large and restless excluded classes. But the laborer's equity is recognized, and his just share is a matter of time, intelligence, and skillful negotiation.

Such nations it is that rule the modern world. Their national bond is no mere sentimental patriotism, loyalty, or ancestor-worship. It is increased wealth, power, and luxury for all classes on a scale the world never saw before. Never before was the average citizen of England, France, and Germany so rich, with such splendid prospects of greater riches.

Whence comes this new wealth and on what does its accumulation depend? It comes primarily from the darker nations of the world—Asia and Africa, South and Central America, the West Indies and the islands of the South Seas. There are still, we may well believe, many parts of white countries like Russia and North America, not to mention Europe itself, where the older exploitation still holds. But the knell has sounded faint and far, even there. In the lands of darker folk, however, no knell has sounded. Chinese, East Indians, Negroes, and South American Indians, are by common consent for governance by white folk and economic subjection to them. To the furtherance of this highly profitable economic dictum has been brought every available resource of science and religion. Thus arises the astonishing doctrine of the natural inferiority of most men to the few, and the interpretation of "Christian brotherhood" as meaning anything that one of the "brothers" may at any time want it to mean. . . .

What, then, are we to do, who desire peace and the civilization of all men? Hitherto the peace movement has confined itself chiefly to figures about the cost of war and platitudes on humanity. What do nations care about the cost of war, if by spending a few hundred millions in steel and gunpowder they can gain a thousand millions in diamonds and cocoa?

How can love of humanity appeal as a motive to nations whose love of luxury is built on the inhuman exploitation of human beings, and who, especially in recent years, have been taught to regard these human beings as inhuman? I appealed to the last meeting of peace societies in St. Louis, saying, "Should you not discuss racial prejudice as a prime cause of war?" The secretary was sorry but was unwilling to introduce controversial matters!

We, then, who want peace, must remove the real causes of war. We have extended gradually our conception of democracy beyond our social class to all social classes in our nation; we have gone further and extended our democratic ideals not simply to all classes of our nation, but to those of other nations of our blood and lineage—to what we call "European" civilization. If we want real peace and lasting culture, however, we must go further. We must extend the democratic ideal to the yellow, brown and black peoples.

7

CHARLES T. MAGILL

Not One Person of Color Had a Vote

1920

Most of the territory in the Caribbean and Pacific obtained by the United States around 1898 had previously been claimed by European empires. Prior histories of colonization as well as ongoing migrations across imperial boundaries can be found, for example, in the U.S. Virgin Islands (the largest of which are St. Thomas, St. Croix, and St. John), purchased from Denmark in 1917. This article, written for the largely African American readership of the Chicago Defender, *reports on a talk by St. Croix labor leader David Hamilton Jackson. The Manhood Movement that Jackson alludes to was also known as the New Negro Movement. It helped lay the groundwork for the border-crossing black empowerment movement led by Marcus Garvey.*

Charles T. Magill, "Conditions in Virgin Island Intolerable," *Chicago Defender*, October 2, 1920.

Two thousand whites, or 3 per cent of the total Virgin Islands' population, completely dominate the 20,000 full blooded persons of color and the 4,500 persons of mixed blood, who go to make up the population of the three islands—St. Croix, St. Thomas and St. John.

D. Hamilton Jackson, educational secretary of the Labor, Social and Reform Party (Manhood Movement), and editor of the *St. Croix Herald*, in an interview with *The Chicago Defender* correspondent, declared that the time was rapidly coming when these intolerable conditions would be entirely obliterated.

Mr. Jackson, who was formerly president of the labor party, will remain in this country one year studying American institutions. He will also try to induce the coming congress to pass legislation that will be helpful to his people; some of the things much needed being a water works system and more adequate hospitals. At present the Virgin Islands have absolutely no water system, the only water obtainable being that caught from the rain.

The noted islander, a tall, finely formed man, who speaks excellent English, explained that the planters, who are the land owners, hold all the public offices and make all the laws. One of these laws is that in order to vote, one must have an income of $300 annually. Before the days of the manhood movement, not one person of color had a vote; today, 450 of them have qualified. In the old days the hated planters, all descendants of the cruel Danish slaveholders, paid the laborers wages of 15 or 20 cents per day. This wage scale existed up until 1915, the year Jackson succeeded in getting the laborers organized. Today, the workers earn not less than $1.00 per day, a good sum in those islands.

The complete domination by these planters, who number not more than 2,000 of the Colonial Council, the law making body, is slowly being shaken. This council is made up of eighteen members, thirteen of whom are elected, and five appointed. The appointed five are supposed to look after the interest of the disenfranchised. Since they, too, however, are white, they pay no attention to those for whom they are appointed. Under the present rule of Rear Admiral James Oman, governor of the Virgin Islands, better conditions are being brought about. In fact, said Mr. Jackson, since becoming an American possession, and since getting rid of the first American governor, James H. Oliver of Georgia, it can be truthfully said that Virgin Island conditions in general are better. Governor Oman, he said, has been eminently fair, and in so far as he could, has caused the white planters to cease their tyranny over the natives. Under his ruling, direct access to him personally may be had by any one with a grievance. Formerly the planters would cause the arrest of a native, perhaps, because he objected to harsh treatment, [haul] the unfortunate before one of the white magistrates and have him unceremoniously committed to jail. Today, Admiral Oman has caused to be substituted for this procedure a trial by jury.

Speaking of the British possessions, Mr. Jackson said that conditions there are infinitely worse than on the Virgin Islands. There, said the manhood leader, natives are practically living in slavery, since the peonage system is in full bloom, and the natives are wretchedly poor, rarely receiving more than a shilling a day for their labor. Many of the Virgin Islanders are native British West Indians, coming there to escape the frightful conditions imposed on them under English rule in their own country.

Concluding the interview, Mr. Jackson predicted a better day coming for the Virgin Islands. With continued prosperity, enabling more of the people of color to vote, it will soon be possible to elect one of their own kind to the Colonial Council, and thus share in the law making.

2

Missionary Endeavors

8

MARY AND MARGARET W. LEITCH

The Women of Heathen Lands Need the Gospel
1890

For seven years starting in 1880, Mary and Margaret W. Leitch worked as Protestant missionaries in Jaffna, Ceylon (now known as Sri Lanka). In this essay, the sisters recall the life and work of Eliza Agnew, a New Yorker by birth who became an overseas missionary in 1839. Although married women had previously gone with their husbands as missionaries to the British crown colony of Ceylon, Agnew was the first single woman to do so. The Tamils referred to in the piece are a Hindu people with a rich literary tradition stretching back to the sixth century CE.

One day the teacher in a day-school in New York City, while giving a lesson in geography, pointed out to her pupils the heathen and the Christian lands, and she must have spoken some very earnest words to them, for then and there a little girl, eight years of age, named Eliza Agnew, resolved that, if it were God's will, she would be a missionary when she grew up, and help to tell the heathen about Jesus. She never forgot this resolve. Until she was thirty years of age she was detained at home, because there were near relations who needed her care. But when she had reached that age, and her dear ones had been called away from earth to heaven, she was free to leave her home, and she went as a missionary to Ceylon.

Mary and Margaret W. Leitch, *Seven Years in Ceylon: Stories of Mission Life* (New York: American Tract Society, 1890), 116–20.

Some years before this, when the first missionaries reached North Ceylon, they could not find, among the more than 300,000 people there, a single native woman or girl who could read. There were a few men and boys who could read, but the people did not think it worth while to teach the girls. They said, "What are girls good for, excepting to cook food?" &c. "Besides," they said, "girls could not learn to read any more than sheep." The missionaries said to them, "You are mistaken. Girls can learn to read as well as boys." So they opened mission day-schools not only for boys, but for girls also.

Though the parents willingly allowed their sons to attend these schools, they were very unwilling to let their daughters remain long enough to receive an education, as it was common for parents to give their daughters in marriage when they were only ten or twelve years of age. Seeing this, one of the missionary ladies wished to commence a boarding-school for girls. She wished to have the native girls separated from the influences of their heathen homes, and brought under daily Christian influence. But none of the people would send their daughters to her.

One day there were two little girls playing in the flower-garden in front of the missionary's house at Oodooville. Ceylon is in the tropics, only nine degrees north of the equator. In North Ceylon there are two seasons, the "*wet*" and the "*dry*." The dry season lasts nine months, and during that time there is scarcely any rain; but in the wet season, November, December, and January, it rains nearly every day, and sometimes the rain falls in torrents—between nine and ten inches have been known to fall in twenty-four hours. While these two little girls were playing, there came on a heavy shower of rain, and as they had not time to go home, they ran for shelter into the missionary's house. It continued to rain all that afternoon and evening, and the little girls became very hungry and began to cry. The missionary lady gave them bread and bananas. The younger girl ate, but the older girl refused to eat. After a time, when the rain ceased a little, the parents went to look for their daughters. They had supposed they would be in some neighbor's house, but found them in that of the missionary. When they heard that the younger one had eaten, they were very angry, for they said, "She has lost caste." They found fault with the missionary lady, and the mother said, "You have given my child food, and it has broken caste and is polluted, and now we shall not be able to arrange a marriage for it. What shall we do? You may take the child and bring it up."

The missionary lady had been wishing for native girls to come to her, whom she might educate in a boarding-school, and here was a mother actually saying she might take her daughter, so the missionary lady thought that perhaps this was the Lord's way of enabling her to start the boarding-school. She took the little girl, fed and clothed her, and began teaching her the 247 letters of the Tamil alphabet. She sprinkled a little sand on the floor of the veranda, and taught the child to write the letters in the sand. By-and-by, some of the playmates of this little girl came to see her, and when they saw her writing the letters in the sand, they thought that this was some kind of new play, and they also wanted to learn. The Tamil children have good memories, and in a very short time they committed to memory the 247 letters of the alphabet and were able to read. Their parents seeing this, and that the little girl was well cared for and happy, soon began to entrust more of their daughters to the care of the missionary lady. This was the beginning of the Oodooville Girls' Boarding-school, which was, perhaps, the first boarding-school for girls in a heathen land, having been commenced in 1824.

After Miss Agnew went to Ceylon, she became the head of this boarding-school. She remained in Ceylon for forty-three years without once going home for a rest or a change. . . .

In the Oodooville Girls' Boarding-school, she taught the children, and even some of the grandchildren, of her first pupils. More than 1000 girls have studied under her. She was much loved by the girls, who each regarded her as a mother, and she was poetically called by the people, "The mother of a thousand daughters." During the years she taught in the school more than 600 girls went out from it as Christians. We believe that no girl having taken its whole course has ever graduated as a heathen. Most of these girls came from heathen homes and heathen villages, but in this school they learned of Christ and of His great love, and surrendered their young hearts to Him.

Miss Agnew lived with us in our home the last two years of her life, when she had grown feeble and was no longer able to retain the charge of the boarding-school. We felt her presence in our home to be a daily blessing.

Near the close of her brief illness, and when we knew that she had not many hours to live, one of the missionaries present asked her if he should offer prayer. She eagerly assented. He asked, "Is there anything for which you would like me specially to pray?" She replied, *"Pray for the women of Jaffna, that they may come to Christ."* She had no thought about herself. . . . At the very time when she was asking prayers for the women of Jaffna, every room in our house was filled with native Christian women who, when girls, had been her pupils, and they were praying for her—that if it were the Lord's will to take her then to Himself, He would save her from suffering and pain. God heard their prayer, and she passed away like one going into a sweet sleep. The attendance at the funeral service was very large. Many native pastors, catechists, teachers, lawyers, Government officials and others, the leading men of

Jaffna Peninsula, who had married girls trained in the Oodooville Girls' Boarding-school, came to the funeral service, bringing their wives and children. As we looked over that large audience and saw everywhere faces full of love and eyes full of tears, and knew that to hundreds of homes she had brought the light and hope and joy of the Gospel, we could not help thinking *how precious a life consecrated to Christ may be.*

In hundreds of villages in Ceylon and India there is just such a work waiting to be done by Christian young women as that which, with God's blessing, Miss Agnew accomplished in the Jaffna Peninsula. Heathen lands are open to-day as they have never been open before. The women of heathen lands need the Gospel. The stronghold of heathenism is in the homes. Many of the men in India have to some extent lost faith in their old superstitious creeds, but the women, who are secluded in the homes, cling to the heathen worship. What else can they do? They must cling to something, and the majority of them have not heard of Christ. They are teaching the children to perform the heathen ceremonies, to sing the songs in praise of the heathen gods, and thus they are moulding the habits of thought of the coming generation. Some one has truly said, "If we are to win India for Christ, we must lay our hands on the hands that rock the cradles, and teach Christian songs to the lips that sing the lullabies, and if we can win the *mothers* of India to Christ, her *future sons* will soon be brought to fall at the feet of their Redeemer."

9

QUEEN LILIUOKALANI

The "Missionary Party" Took the Law into Its Own Hands

1898

This document comes from the autobiography of Queen Liliuokalani (also spelled Lili'uokalani), the last reigning monarch of the kingdom of Hawai'i. In this section of her autobiography, Liliuokalani discusses the reign of her brother, David Kalākaua, who served as king from 1874 until his death in 1891. He presided over an 1875 treaty that allowed Hawai'ian

Queen Liliuokalani, *Hawaii's Story by Hawaii's Queen Liliuokalani* (Boston: Lee and Shepard, 1898), 177–81.

agricultural goods to be imported tax-free into the United States. Yet the powerful white plantation owners who benefitted most from this treaty forced Kalākaua to sign the "Bayonet Constitution" of 1887. This constitution placed executive power in the hands of the king's planter-dominated cabinet and disenfranchised much of Hawai'i's indigenous population. The "missionary party" mentioned in this document took its name from its many supporters who had grown up in missionary families.

For many years our sovereigns had welcomed the advice of, and given full representations in their government and councils to, American residents who had cast in their lot with our people, and established industries on the Islands. As they became wealthy, and acquired titles to lands through the simplicity of our people and their ignorance of values and of the new land laws, their greed and their love of power proportionately increased; and schemes for aggrandizing themselves still further, or for avoiding the obligations which they had incurred to us, began to occupy their minds. So the mercantile element, as embodied in the Chamber of Commerce, the sugar planters, and the proprietors of the "missionary" stores, formed a distinct political party, called the "down-town" party, whose purpose was to minimize or entirely subvert other interests, and especially the prerogatives of the crown, which, based upon ancient custom and the authority of the island chiefs, were the sole guaranty of our nationality. Although settled among us, and drawing their wealth from our resources, they were alien to us in their customs and ideas respecting government, and desired above all things the extension of their power, and to carry out their own special plans of advancement, and to secure their own personal benefit. It may be true that they really believed us unfit to be trusted to administer the growing wealth of the Islands in a safe and proper way. But if we manifested any incompetency, it was in not foreseeing that *they* would be bound by no obligations, by honor, or by oath of allegiance, should an opportunity arise for seizing our country, and bringing it under the authority of the United States.

Kalakaua valued the commercial and industrial prosperity of his kingdom highly. He sought honestly to secure it for every class of people, alien or native, in his dominions, making it second only to the advancement of morals and education. If he believed in the divine right of kings, and the distinctions of hereditary nobility, it was not alone from the prejudices of birth and native custom, but because he was able to perceive that even the most enlightened nations of the earth have not as yet been able to replace them with a ruling class equally able, patriotic, or disinterested. I say this with all reverence for the form of government and the social order existing in the United States, whose workings have, for more than a century, excited the interest of the world; not the interest of the common people only, but of nobles, rulers, and kings. Kalakaua's highest and most earnest desire was to be a true sovereign, the chief servant of a happy, prosperous, and progressive people. He regarded himself as the responsible arbiter of clashing interests, and his own breast as the ordained meeting-place of the spears of political contention. He was rightly jealous of his prerogatives, because they were responsibilities which no civic body in his kingdom could safely undertake to administer. He freely gave his personal efforts to the securing of a reciprocity treaty with the United States, and sought the co-operation of that great and powerful nation, because he was persuaded it would enrich, or benefit, not one class, but, in a greater or less degree, all his subjects.

His interviews with General Grant,[1] his investigations into the labor problems, which the success of the Hawaiian plantations demanded, were all means to the same end,—an increase in domestic prosperity. He succeeded, and the joy of the majority was great. The planters were elated, the merchants were encouraged, money flowed into their pockets, bankrupt firms became wealthy, sugar companies declared fabulous dividends; the prosperity for which my brother had so faithfully worked he most abundantly secured for his people, especially for those of foreign birth, or missionary ancestry, who had become permanent residents of Hawaii.

The king did not accomplish these things without some native opposition; although it was respectful and deferent to his decision, as the ideas and customs of our people require. Some foresaw that this treaty with the United States might become the entering wedge for the loss of our independence. What would be the consequences should the Islands acquire too great a commercial attraction, too large a foreign population and interests? Would not these interests demand the protection of a flag backed by a great military or naval power? But Kalakaua, aware that under the provisions of international law no nation could attack us without cause, and relying on the established policy of our great ally, the United States, fully assured that no colonial scheme would find acceptation there, boldly adventured upon the effort which so greatly increased the wealth and importance of his kingdom,—a wealth which has, however, owing to circumstances which he could not then foresee, and which none of

---

[1] General Ulysses S. Grant, eighteenth president of the United States. The interviews pertained to the 1875 treaty between the United States and Hawai'i.

his loyal counselors even dreamed of, now gone almost wholly into the pockets of aliens and foes.

For years the "missionary party" had, by means of controlling the cabinets appointed by the king, kept itself in power. Its leaders were constantly intriguing to make the ministry their tool, or to have in its organization a power for carrying out their own special plans, and securing their own personal benefit. And now, without any provocation on the part of the king, having matured their plans in secret, the men of foreign birth rose one day *en masse*, called a public meeting, and forced the king, without any appeal to the suffrages of the people, to sign a constitution of their own preparation, a document which deprived the sovereign of all power, made him a mere tool in their hands, and practically took away the franchise from the Hawaiian race. This constitution was never in any way ratified, either by the people, or by their representatives, even after violence had procured the king's signature to it. Contrary entirely to the intent of the prior constitution drawn by a Hawaiian monarch (under which for twenty-three years the nation had been conducted to prosperity), this draft of 1887 took all power from the ruler, and meant that from that day the "missionary party" took the law into its own hands.

10

ZITKALA-ŠA [GERTRUDE SIMMONS]

I Had Been Uprooted from My Mother, Nature, and God

1900

Zitkala-Ša is the pen name taken by Gertrude Simmons, a Yankton Sioux from South Dakota, educated from the age of eight at a Quaker-run boarding school. Such schools aimed to Americanize Native American children by separating them from their families and tribal culture. The schools' founders believed that assimilation could be achieved within the students' lifetimes, rather than across the generations. As Richard Henry Pratt,

Zitkala-Ša, "An Indian Teacher among Indians," *Atlantic Monthly* 85 (March 1900): 385–86.

who recruited Sioux children to his boarding school in Carlisle, Pennsylvania, put it, the schools would "kill the Indian . . . and save the man." The parents who allowed boarding school agents to take their children viewed the matter differently: They regarded education as a means to recover lost land and resist colonial policies. As a young adult, Simmons taught at Carlisle. This essay starts with an account of a visit home before Simmons left teaching to become a writer and political activist. (For another account of boarding school education, see Document 43.)

One black night mother and I sat alone in the dim starlight, in front of our wigwam. We were facing the river, as we talked about the shrinking limits of the village. She told me about the poverty-stricken white settlers, who lived in caves dug in the long ravines of the high hills across the river.

A whole tribe of broad-footed white beggars had rushed hither to make claims on those wild lands. Even as she was telling this I spied a small glimmering light in the bluffs.

"That is a white man's lodge where you see the burning fire," she said. Then, a short distance from it, only a little lower than the first, was another light. As I became accustomed to the night, I saw more and more twinkling lights, here and there, scattered all along the wide black margin of the river.

Still looking toward the distant firelight, my mother continued: "My daughter, beware of the paleface. It was the cruel paleface who caused the death of your sister and your uncle, my brave brother. It is this same paleface who offers in one palm the holy papers, and with the other gives a holy baptism of firewater. He is the hypocrite who reads with one eye, 'Thou shalt not kill,' and with the other gloats upon the sufferings of the Indian race.' Then suddenly discovering a new fire in the bluffs, she exclaimed, "Well, well, my daughter, there is the light of another white rascal!"

She sprang to her feet, and, standing firm beside her wigwam, she sent a curse upon those who sat around the hated white man's light. Raising her right arm forcibly into line with her eye, she threw her whole might into her doubled fist as she shot it vehemently at the strangers. Long she held her outstretched fingers toward the settler's lodge, as if an invisible power passed from them to the evil at which she aimed.

. . . Leaving my mother, I returned to the school in the East. As months passed over me, I slowly comprehended that the large army of white teachers in Indian schools had a larger missionary creed than I had suspected.

It was one which included self-preservation quite as much as Indian education. When I saw an opium-eater holding a position as teacher of Indians, I did not understand what good was expected, until a Christian in power replied that this pumpkin-colored creature had a feeble mother to support. An inebriate paleface sat stupid in a doctor's chair, while Indian patients carried their ailments to untimely graves, because his fair wife was dependent upon him for her daily food.

I find it hard to count that white man a teacher who tortured an ambitious Indian youth by frequently reminding the brave changeling that he was nothing but a "government pauper."

Though I burned with indignation upon discovering on every side instances no less shameful than those I have mentioned, there was no present help. Even the few rare ones who have worked nobly for my race were powerless to choose workmen like themselves. To be sure, a man was sent from the Great Father to inspect Indian schools, but what he saw was usually the students' sample work *made* for exhibition. I was nettled by this sly cunning of the workmen who hoodwinked the Indian's pale Father at Washington.

My illness, which prevented the conclusion of my college course, together with my mother's stories of the encroaching frontier settlers, left me in no mood to strain my eyes in searching for latent good in my white co-workers.

At this stage of my own evolution, I was ready to curse men of small capacity for being the dwarfs their God had made them. In the process of my education I had lost all consciousness of the nature world about me. Thus, when a hidden rage took me to the small white-walled prison which I then called my room, I unknowingly turned away from my one salvation.

Alone in my room, I sat like the petrified Indian woman of whom my mother used to tell me. I wished my heart's burdens would turn me to unfeeling stone. But alive, in my tomb, I was destitute!

For the white man's papers I had given up my faith in the Great Spirit. For these same papers I had forgotten the healing in trees and brooks. On account of my mother's simple view of life, and my lack of any, I gave her up, also. I made no friends among the race of people I loathed. Like a slender tree, I had been uprooted from my mother, nature, and God. I was shorn of my branches, which had waved in sympathy and love for home and friends. The natural coat of bark which had protected my oversensitive nature was scraped off to the very quick.

Now a cold bare pole I seemed to be, planted in a strange earth.

11

EDWIN H. CONGER

The Missionaries Have Some Twenty Guns

1900

*In 1889, close to five hundred U.S. missionaries were living in China,
aided by about fourteen hundred Chinese helpers; by 1899, there were
over a thousand U.S. missionaries in China. The spreading presence of
Christian missionaries sparked antiforeign sentiments, which coalesced
in the Spirit Boxer movement. (This was a Western name that reflected
the Boxers' ritual use of martial arts. In Chinese, the Boxers were known
as the Righteous Fists of Harmony.) The Boxers urged the Chinese people
to preserve traditional values by driving foreigners out. In the summer
of 1900, Boxers attacked foreign missionaries and their Chinese associates and held the foreign legations in Peking under siege for three weeks.
An allied force that included several thousand U.S. soldiers put down
the uprising. Edwin H. Conger, the top U.S. diplomatic representative
to China, sent this dispatch to Secretary of State John Hay.*

SIR: I have the honor to confirm herewith the telegraphic correspon-
dence with the Department since June 5, and to say that the situation
here has been daily growing worse.

The Chinese Government has done nothing toward suppressing the
Boxers except to send their friends out to parley with them.

They have ever since the 6th instant had absolute possession and
control of the whole country surrounding the city. The railroad has been
open but one day. They have killed many native Christians, at least 40
belonging to the American missions, and burned numerous chapels.
Only yesterday they burned the college of the American Board Mission at Tung-chow together with all their homes, from which on the
7th instant all had been compelled to flee to this city, leaving practically everything behind them. This was done by the Chinese soldiers

"Mr. Conger to Mr. Hay," *Papers Relating to the Foreign Relations of the United States,
with the Annual Message of the President* (Washington, D.C.: Government Printing
Office, 1902), 144.

themselves, or else in their presence and without their opposition. They have burned the summer residences of the British legation and all the houses of the American Board, Methodist and Presbyterian missions, at the Western Hills. On the 9th were burned all the buildings of the foreign race course just outside the city walls.

We have four American missions and one international under the control of an American, widely scattered in this large city. They each wanted a guard, which was impossible, but I told them they ought to remain at their missions as long as possible (for desertions here always invite trouble), and when it became necessary to abandon them, if they would all assemble in one compound I would furnish them a guard.

On the 7th it was thought best by all to gather in the Methodist compound, which is the largest, the easiest to defend, and the nearest to the legation.

There are now 70 Americans there, 51 of whom are women and children. They have a guard of 20 marines, and the missionaries have some 20 guns and revolvers besides. If it becomes necessary they can all get inside of a large church and defend themselves against quite a formidable siege.

We have assembled in the legation compound 32 Americans, 25 of whom are women and children, with a guard of 35 marines and a rapid-fire gun.

On the 8th the conditions were so ominous that some of us asked the Tsungli Yamen[1] for permission to bring additional guards, which was refused.

On the 9th the Emperor and the Empress Dowager returned to the city from the summer palace. The Tsungli Yamen was so excited, declared the Government so helpless, and the Chinese soldiers were so insulting and threatening that I wired Admiral Kempff[2] that railroad communication ought to be opened and a movement in force made on Pekin, if possible. The British minister wired the English admiral in the same tenor.

---

[1] The Chinese foreign office.
[2] Rear Admiral Louis Kempff, commander of the U.S. Asiatic Fleet.

3

Co-opting the Cuban Revolution

12

JOSÉ MARTÍ AND MÁXIMO GÓMEZ

For the Good of America and the World

1895

José Martí and General Máximo Gómez penned this manifesto in Gómez's hacienda in the Dominican Republic before embarking for Cuba to begin the third struggle for independence. They hoped this manifesto would help them build a multiracial and cross-class coalition. Before enlisting in the revolutionary army, Martí had made his living as a writer. In 1892, he founded the Cuban Revolutionary Party, which called for an independent, democratic Cuba dedicated to racial equality and economic justice. Gómez served as commander in chief of the Cuban army. Even though both leaders signed their names to this document, the phrasing suggests that Martí played the major role in drafting it.

The revolution for independence, begun at Yara[1] after glorious and bloody preparations, has led Cuba into another period of war, by virtue of the command and agreements of the Revolutionary Party abroad and on the island, and of the exemplary brotherhood in the Party of all the elements dedicated to the country's emancipation and security, for the good of America and the world. The elected representatives of the

[1]A small town in eastern Cuba.

José Martí and Máximo Gómez, *Manifesto of Montecristi*, foreword by Armando Hart (Havana: Oficina de Publicaciones del Consejo de Estado Oficina del Programa Martiano, 2000), 13–19.

revolution which is today confirmed, recognize and respect their duty to repeat to the country its precise objectives. . . .

[The war] . . . must be the disciplined product of the resolve of men of integrity who, in the serenity of experience, have once again determined to face the dangers they know. It must be the product of a sincere brotherhood of Cubans of the most diverse origins, convinced that it is in the conquest of freedom rather than in abject despair that they are acquiring the virtues necessary to the maintenance of that war.

The war is not directed against the Spaniard, for he, in the security of his children and out of respect for the country they will acquire, will himself be able to enjoy, respected and even loved, the freedom that will crush only those who improvidently leave the path. Nor will the war be born of disorder, alien to the tried and tested moderation of the Cuban spirit. And it will not be born of oppression. Those who promoted it, and can still make their voices heard, declare in its name and before the country their freedom from all hatred, their brotherly indulgence toward timid or mistaken Cubans, their radical respect for man's integrity in combat and his energy in supporting the republic. They declare their certainty that the war can be organized in such a way that it contains the redemption inspiring it, the relationship in which one nation must live with others, and the reality of which it is made. The instigators are determined to respect the neutral and honest Spaniard, and see that he is respected, both during the war and after it is over, as well as to be merciful toward repentance, and inflexible only toward vice, crime, and inhumanity. In the resumption of Cuba's war, the revolution sees no reason for merriment that might impede an impulsive heroism; it does see the responsibilities that should concern the builders of nations. . . .

Today cowardice might have to make use of another fear, on the pretext of prudence: an unreasoning fear of the Negro race, never justified in Cuba. The revolution, with its abundance of martyrs and of generous and obedient fighters, indignantly contradicts — as the long testing period of the communities abroad and the truce on the island is contradicting — the charge that the Negro race is a threat, a charge wickedly made by the beneficiaries of the Spanish regime in order to stir up fear of the revolution. In Cuba there are now Cubans of both colors who have put out of their minds forever, with the emancipatory war and the work in which together they are becoming proficient, the hatred with which slavery was able to divide them. Bitterness and a changed state of social relations, resulting from the sudden transformation of the foreigner into a "native," are less important than the Cuban white man's sincere esteem for the kindred spirit, the laborious culture, the free man's fervor, and the amiable character of his Negro compatriot. And if the Negro race were to produce some filthy demagogues or avid souls, whose own impatience were to stir up that of their color, or in whom compassion for their own people might lead to injustice toward others—then with its gratitude and practical wisdom, its love of country, its conviction that it is necessary to deprive of authority the still prevailing opinion that the race is incapable of these qualities, and with the possession of all that is real in human rights, and with the enjoyment of and strong respect for all that is just and generous in the Cuban white man, the Negro race itself would eradicate the Negro danger single-handedly, with no help from the white man needed. The Cuban Negro's integrity and intelligence have been patently proved. This the revolution knows and proclaims, and so do the Cubans living abroad. The Cuban Negro has no schools of anger there, just as in the war there was not a single case of undue pride or insubordination. The republic against which the Negro has never rebelled rests safely upon his shoulders. Only those who hate the Negro can see any hate in him, and only those who trafficked in similar unjust fear in order to control, with an undesirable authority, the hands that might rise to the task of expelling the corrupting occupant from Cuban soil.

13

JOHN M. THURSTON

We Must Act!

1898

Under the command of General Valeriano Weyler, the Spanish army forced rural Cubans into concentration camps to prevent them from aiding guerrillas in the countryside. The result: hunger, disease, and death, made worse by the Cuban revolutionaries' destruction of farms and livestock. As many as 170,000 Cuban civilians died in the conflict, which left the economic infrastructure of the country in shambles. Senator John M. Thurston, a Republican from Nebraska, was part of a congressional delegation that

Remarks of Senator Thurston, *Congressional Record*, 55th Cong., 2nd Sess., March 24, 1898, 3162–65.

visited Cuba in March 1898. Upon his return, he spoke on Cuban affairs before the U.S. Senate. The "silent lips" he invokes in his opening remarks are those of his wife, Martha Thurston, who died of a fever in Cuba.

Mr. THURSTON. Mr. President, I am here by command of silent lips to speak once and for all upon the Cuban situation. I trust that no one has expected anything sensational from me. God forbid that the bitterness of a personal loss should induce me to color in the slightest degree the statement that I feel it my duty to make. I shall endeavor to be honest, conservative, and just. I have no purpose to stir the public passion to any action not necessary and imperative to meet the duties and necessities of American responsibility, Christian humanity, and national honor. I would shirk this task if I could, but I dare not. I can not satisfy my conscience except by speaking, and speaking now. . . .

After three years of warfare and the use of 225,000 Spanish troops, Spain has lost control of every foot of Cuba not surrounded by an actual intrenchment and protected by a fortified picket line.

She holds possession with her armies of the fortified seaboard towns, not because the insurgents could not capture many of them, but because they are under the virtual protection of Spanish war ships, with which the revolutionists can not cope.

The revolutionists are in absolute and almost peaceful possession of nearly one-half of the island, including the eastern provinces of Santiago de Cuba and Puerto Principe. In those provinces they have an established form of government, levy and collect taxes, maintain armies, and generally levy a tax or tribute upon the principal plantations in the other provinces, and, as is commonly believed, upon the entire railway system of the island. . . .

The Spanish soldiers have not been paid for some months, and in my judgment they, of all the people on the earth, will most gladly welcome any result which would permit them to return to their homes in Spain.

The pictures in the American newspapers of the starving reconcentrados[1] are true. They can all be duplicated by the thousands. I never saw, and please God I may never again see, so deplorable a sight as the reconcentrados in the suburbs of Matanzas. I can never forget to my dying day the hopeless anguish in their despairing eyes. Huddled about their little bark huts, they raised no voice of appeal to us for alms as we went among them.

---

[1] Concentration camp inmates.

There was almost no begging by the reconcentrados themselves. The streets of the cities are full of beggars of all ages and all conditions, but they are almost wholly of the residents of the cities and largely of the professional-beggar class. The reconcentrados—men, women, and children—stand silent, famishing with hunger. Their only appeal comes from their sad eyes, through which one looks as through an open window into their agonizing souls. . . .

The Government of Spain has not and will not appropriate one dollar to save these people. They are now being attended and nursed and administered to by the charity of the United States. Think of the spectacle! We are feeding these citizens of Spain; we are nursing their sick; we are saving such as can be saved, and yet there are those who still say it is right for us to send food, but we must keep hands off. I say that the time has come when muskets ought to go with the food. . . .

Twice within the last two years I have voted for a resolution according the rights of belligerents to the Cuban revolutionists.

I believed at those times, I still believe, that such a recognition on our part would have enabled the Cuban patriots to have achieved independence for themselves; that it would have given them such a standing in the money markets of the world, such rights on the sea, such flag on the land, that ere this the independence of Cuba would have been secured, and that without cost or loss of blood or treasure to the people of the United States. But that time has passed; it is too late to talk about resolutions according belligerent rights; and mere resolutions recognizing the independence of the Cuban Republic would avail but little. . . .

The time for action has, then, come. No greater reason for it can exist to-morrow than exists to-day. Every hour's delay only adds another chapter to the awful story of misery and death. Only one power can intervene—the United States of America. Ours is the one great nation of the New World, the mother of American republics. She holds a position of trust and responsibility toward the peoples and the affairs of the whole Western Hemisphere.

It was her glorious example which inspired the patriots of Cuba to raise the flag of liberty in her eternal hills. We can not refuse to accept this responsibility which the God of the universe has placed upon us as the one great power in the New World. We must act! . . .

Mr. President, there is only one action possible, if any is taken; that is, intervention for the independence of the island; intervention that means the landing of an American army on Cuban soil, the deploying of an American fleet off Habana;[2] intervention which says to Spain, Leave the island,

---

[2]The Spanish word for Havana.

withdraw your soldiers, leave the Cubans, these brothers of ours in the New World, to form and carry on government for themselves. Such intervention on our part would not of itself be war. It would undoubtedly lead to war. But if war came it would come by act of Spain in resistance of the liberty and the independence of the Cuban people. . . .

Mr. President, there are those who say that the affairs of Cuba are not the affairs of the United States, who insist that we can stand idly by and see that island devastated and depopulated, its business interests destroyed, its commercial intercourse with us cut off, its people starved, degraded, and enslaved. It may be the naked legal right of the United States to stand thus idly by.

I have the legal right to pass along the street and see a helpless dog stamped into the earth under the heels of a ruffian. I can pass by and say that is not my dog. I can sit in my comfortable parlor with my loved ones gathered about me, and through my plate-glass window see a fiend outraging a helpless woman near by, and I can legally say this is no affair of mine — it is not happening on my premises; and I can turn away and take my little ones in my arms, and, with the memory of their sainted mother in my heart, look up to the motto on the wall and read, "God bless our home."

But if I do, I am a coward and a cur unfit to live, and, God knows, unfit to die.

14

THE NEW ENGLAND WOMAN SUFFRAGE ASSOCIATION

Women Can and Do Fight

1898

As war with Spain began to seem imminent, a number of women offered their support to the U.S. government. The women who served as military nurses laid the groundwork for the Army Corps of Nurses, founded in 1901. Although some women believed that vigorous support for the war effort would advance their claims for full citizenship, others expressed

---

"Cubans and Women," *The Woman's Column*, May 21, 1898.

concerns that the war would set back the women's suffrage cause. While the New England suffragists who passed the following resolutions focused on their own rights as citizens, suffrage supporter Rachel Foster Avery drew attention to the rights of Cuban women. "When Cuba shall be free," she wrote, "does that mean that Cuban men shall be free to arrange a government for Cuban women?"

At the annual meeting of the New England Woman Suffrage Association, May 17, resolutions were adopted as follows:

Whereas, the Cuban struggle for independence has led to a strong reaffirmation of the right of all people to self-government; and whereas, American women are better qualified for self-government by education than most of the Cubans; therefore,

Resolved, That while we earnestly desire freedom and self-government for the Cubans, the claim of their American sisters should not be forgotten.

Whereas, a large proportion of our young volunteers have been rejected as physically disqualified; and whereas, it is not proposed to disfranchise either them or the old and infirm men, the halt, the lame and the blind, who could under no circumstances go to war; therefore,

Resolved, That this illustrates anew the fallacy of the argument that suffrage must be conditioned on the power to perform military service. And

Whereas, for the past three years Cuban women have been fighting side by side with their husbands and brothers against the Spaniards; therefore,

Resolved, That we call attention to the fact that in extreme circumstances women can and do fight. As Hon. John D. Long, Secretary of the Navy, said several years ago: "Think of arguing with a sober face against a man whose brains are reduced to such a minimum that he solemnly asserts a woman must not vote because she cannot fight! In the first place, she can fight; in the second, men are largely exempt from military service; and in the third, there is not the remotest relation between firing a musket and casting a ballot."

15

MÁXIMO GÓMEZ

A Tutelage Imposed by Force of Circumstances
1899

*After years of struggle, Cuban forces had to watch their Spanish oppo-
nents surrender to a newly arrived American force that excluded their
own revolutionary army from the proceedings. Along with denigrating
the Cubans' military capabilities, U.S. occupiers disparaged the Cubans'
capacity for self-government. According to one U.S. officer, the insurgents
were "a lot of degenerates . . . no more capable of self-rule than the savages of Africa." As elite white Cubans rose to positions of power during
the occupation, the soldiers who had fought for a more democratic nation
resisted U.S.-backed efforts to impose property and literacy restrictions
on voting. Though a Dominican in origin, General Máximo Gómez had
led the Cuban military since the Ten Years' War of 1868–1878.*

We wanted and depended upon foreign intervention to terminate the war.
This occurred at the most terrible moment of our contest, and resulted
in Spain's defeat. But none of us thought that this extraordinary event
would be followed by a military occupation of the country by our allies,
who treat us as a people incapable of acting for ourselves, and who have
reduced us to obedience, to submission, and to a tutelage imposed by
force of circumstances. This cannot be our ultimate fate after the years
of struggle. . . . Therefore it is necessary to forget past disagreements, to
completely unite all elements and to organize a political party, which is
needed in any country.

It is always said that countries have the government which they merit,
and Cuba will have that to which her heroism entitles her. To-day she
can only have one party, with one object, that of obtaining the aspiration
of years.

We must devote ourselves to pacific labors, gain the respect of the
world, and show that though our war was honorable, our peace must be
more so.

Máximo Gómez, as quoted in "Gomez's Farewell Advice," *New York Times*, June 7, 1899.

We must make useless by our behavior the presence of a strange power in the island, and must assist the Americans to complete the honorable mission which they have been compelled to assume by force of circumstances. This work was not sought by those rich northerners, owners of a continent. I think doubts and suspicions are unjust. We must form immediately a committee or club, to be a nucleus of a Government. This will serve Cuban interests purely, and act as an aid to the intervenors.

I, as one of the first Cubans, although one of our last old soldiers and not far from the grave, without passions or ambitions, call on you with the sincerity of a father, and urge a cessation of the superfluous discussions and the creation of parties of all kinds, which disturb the country and tend to cause anarchy. In this country there should not be one man whom we consider a stranger. To-day we no longer have Autonomists or Conservatives, but only Cubans.

My mission having ended, I will absent myself temporarily to embrace my family but I will return shortly to Cuba, which I love as much as my own land.

My last words for my soldiers are that, as always, where my tent is the Cubans have a friend.

16

HENRY M. TELLER

The People of the Island of Cuba Are, and of Right Ought to Be, Free and Independent

1898

President William McKinley's war message to Congress failed to recognize what the Cubans had been fighting for: an independent republic. To placate Cuba Libre (independent Cuba) supporters, including expatriates living in the United States, the joint resolution authorizing the president to use military force included a provision called the Teller Amendment,

"Public Resolution—No. 21," in U.S. Department of State, *Papers Relating to the Foreign Relations of the United States with the Annual Message of the President Transmitted to Congress, December 5, 1898* (Washington, D.C.: Government Printing Office, 1901), 763.

named after the Colorado senator (Henry M. Teller) who proposed it. Although Teller generally supported U.S. expansion, in offering this amendment he heeded the demands of Colorado's sugar-beet growers, who worried that tariffs on Cuban sugar would be lifted if Cuba were annexed.

Whereas the abhorrent conditions which have existed for more than three years in the island of Cuba, so near our own borders, have shocked the moral sense of the people of the United States, have been a disgrace to civilization, culminating as they have in the destruction of a United States battle ship,[1] with two hundred and sixty-six of its officers and crew, while on a friendly visit in the harbor of Havana, and can not longer be endured, as has been set forth by the President of the United States in his message to Congress of April eleventh, eighteen hundred and ninety-eight, upon which the action of Congress was invited: Therefore,

Resolved by the Senate and House of Representatives of the United States of America in Congress assembled, First. That the people of the island of Cuba are, and of right ought to be, free and independent.

Second. That it is the duty of the United States to demand, and the Government of the United States does hereby demand, that the Government of Spain at once relinquish its authority and government in the island of Cuba, and withdraw its land and naval forces from Cuba and Cuban waters.

Third. That the President of the United States be, and he hereby is, directed and empowered to use the entire land and naval forces of the United States, and to call into the actual service of the United States the militia of the several States, to such extent as may be necessary to carry these resolutions into effect.

Fourth. That the United States hereby disclaims any disposition or intention to exercise sovereignty, jurisdiction, or control over said island, except for the pacification thereof, and asserts its determination, when that is accomplished, to leave the government and control of the island to its people.

[1]The *Maine.*

17

ELIHU ROOT AND ORVILLE PLATT

The United States May Exercise
the Right to Intervene

1901

In 1901, Congress reiterated the promise to "leave the government and control of the island of Cuba to its people." But there was a catch: The Cubans had to affix eight articles to their constitution. These articles, originally drafted by Secretary of War Elihu Root, came to be known as the Platt Amendment, after the senator (Orville Platt) who presented them. Recognizing that the Platt provisions would turn Cuba into a U.S. protectorate, the delegates to Cuba's constitutional convention refused at first to pass them. But when General Leonard Wood made it clear that the Cubans would not have access to the U.S. market for their sugar until they had ratified, the delegates relented in 1903. Realizing that the Platt Amendment had become a rallying cry for Cuban nationalism, President Franklin Delano Roosevelt relinquished all its provisions but the base at Guantánamo as part of his Good Neighbor Policy in the 1930s.

Resolution:

The Constitutional Convention, in conformity with the order from the military governor of the island, dated July 25th, 1900, whereby said convention was convened, has determined to add, and hereby does add, to the Constitution of the Republic of Cuba, adopted on the 21st of February ultimo, the following:

ARTICLE I. The Government of Cuba shall never enter into any treaty or other compact with any foreign power or powers which will impair or tend to impair the independence of Cuba, nor in any way authorize or permit any foreign power or powers to obtain by colonization or for naval or military purposes, or otherwise, lodgement or control over any portion of said island.

Platt Amendment, *Translation of the Proposed Constitution for Cuba, the Official Acceptance of the Platt Amendment, and the Electoral Law*, published by the Division of Insular Affairs, War Department (Washington, D.C.: Government Printing Office, 1901), 23–24.

ART. II. That said Government shall not assume or contract any public debt to pay the interest upon which and to make reasonable sinking-fund provision for the ultimate discharge of which the ordinary revenues of the Island of Cuba, after defraying the current expenses of the Government, shall be inadequate.

ART. III. That the Government of Cuba consents that the United States may exercise the right to intervene for the preservation of Cuban independence, the maintenance of a government adequate for the protection of life, property, and individual liberty, and for discharging the obligations with respect to Cuba imposed by the Treaty of Paris[1] on the United States, now to be assumed and undertaken by the Government of Cuba.

ART. IV. That all the acts of the United States in Cuba during the military occupancy of said island shall be ratified and held as valid, and all rights legally acquired by virtue of said acts shall be maintained and protected.

ART. V. That the Government of Cuba will execute, and, as far as necessary, extend the plans already devised, or other plans to be mutually agreed upon, for the sanitation of the cities of the island, to the end that a recurrence of epidemic and infectious diseases may be prevented, thereby assuring protection to the people and commerce of Cuba, as well as to the commerce of the Southern ports of the United States and the people residing therein.

ART. VI. The island of Pines[2] shall be omitted from the boundaries of Cuba specified in the Constitution, the title of ownership thereof being left to future adjustment by treaty.

ART. VII. To enable the United States to maintain the independence of Cuba, and to protect the people thereof, as well as for its own defence, the Cuban Government will sell or lease to the United States the lands necessary for coaling or naval stations, at certain specified points, to be agreed upon with the President of the United States.

ART. VIII. The Government of Cuba will embody the foregoing provisions in a permanent treaty with the United States.

---

[1] The treaty that ended the war between the United States and Spain.
[2] An island off the southwestern coast of Cuba.

4

Military Conduct

18

THEODORE ROOSEVELT

The Public Promptly Christened Us the "Rough Riders"

1899

Upon the outbreak of the Spanish-American War in April 1898, Theodore Roosevelt resigned his post as assistant secretary of the navy to join the First United States Volunteer Cavalry, nicknamed the Rough Riders. Roosevelt's descriptions of the Rough Riders helped make them national icons and, not incidentally, aided his political ascent—to the governorship of New York, the vice presidency, and then, following the assassination of President McKinley, the White House. More recent accounts of the war have argued that Roosevelt was better at self-promotion than at accurate reporting, especially on the records of the African Americans in the Tenth Cavalry. (See Document 19.)

Raising the Regiment

Within a day or two after it was announced that we were to raise the regiment, we were literally deluged with applications from every quarter of the Union. Without the slightest trouble, so far as men went, we could have raised a brigade or even a division. The difficulty lay in arming, equipping, mounting, and disciplining the men we selected. . . .

Theodore Roosevelt, *The Rough Riders* (New York: Charles Scribner's Sons, 1899), 7–11, 14–16, 20, 143–45.

We drew recruits from Harvard, Yale, Princeton, and many another college; from clubs like the Somerset, of Boston, and Knickerbocker, of New York; and from among the men who belonged neither to club nor to college, but in whose veins the blood stirred with the same impulse which once sent the Vikings over sea. Four of the policemen who had served under me, while I was President of the New York Police Board, insisted on coming—two of them to die, the other two to return unhurt after honorable and dangerous service. It seemed to me that almost every friend I had in every State had some one acquaintance who was bound to go with the Rough Riders, and for whom I had to make a place. . . .

Harvard being my own college, I had such a swarm of applications from it that I could not take one in ten. What particularly pleased me not only in the Harvard but the Yale and Princeton men, and, indeed, in these recruits from the older States generally, was that they did not ask for commissions. With hardly an exception they entered upon their duties as troopers in the spirit which they held to the end, merely endeavoring to show that no work could be too hard, too disagreeable, or too dangerous for them to perform, and neither asking nor receiving any reward in the way of promotion or consideration. . . .

These men formed but a small fraction of the whole. . . . The men from New Mexico, Arizona . . . Oklahoma [and] . . . Indian Territory . . . were the men who made up the bulk of the regiment, and gave it its peculiar character. They came from the Four Territories which yet remained within the boundaries of the United States; that is, from the lands that have been most recently won over to white civilization, and in which the conditions of life are nearest those that obtained on the frontier when there still was a frontier. They were a splendid set of men, these Southwesterners—tall and sinewy, with resolute, weather-beaten faces, and eyes that looked a man straight in the face without flinching. They included in their ranks men of every occupation; but the three types were those of the cow-boy, the hunter, and the mining prospector—the man who wandered hither and thither, killing game for a living, and spending his life in the quest for metal wealth.

In all the world there could be no better material for soldiers than that afforded by these grim hunters of the mountains, these wild rough riders of the plains. They were accustomed to handling wild and savage horses; they were accustomed to following the chase with the rifle, both for sport and as a means of livelihood. Varied though their occupations had been, almost all had, at one time or another, herded cattle and hunted big game. They were hardened to life in the open, and to shifting for themselves under adverse circumstances. They were used, for all their lawless freedom, to the rough discipline of the roundup and the mining company. Some of them came from the small frontier towns; but most were from the wilderness, having left their lonely hunters' cabins and shifting cow-camps to seek new and more stirring adventures beyond the sea. . . .

There was one characteristic and distinctive contingent which could have appeared only in such a regiment as ours. From the Indian Territory there came a number of Indians—Cherokees, Chickasaws, Choctaws, and Creeks. Only a few were of pure blood. The others shaded off until they were absolutely indistinguishable from their white comrades; with whom, it may be mentioned, they all lived on terms of complete equality. . . .

The Cavalry at Santiago

[This part of The Rough Riders *covers the assault on Kettle Hill, in the San Juan range, on the outskirts of Santiago.]*

. . . On the hill-slope immediately around me I had a mixed force composed of members of most of the cavalry regiments, and a few infantrymen. There were about fifty of my Rough Riders with Lieutenants Goodrich and Carr. Among the rest were perhaps a score of colored infantrymen, but, as it happened, at this particular point without any of their officers. No troops could have behaved better than the colored soldiers had behaved so far; but they are, of course, peculiarly dependent upon their white officers. Occasionally they produce non-commissioned officers who can take the initiative and accept the responsibility precisely like the best class of whites; but this cannot be expected normally, nor is it fair to expect it. With the colored troops there should always be some of their own officers; whereas, with the white regulars, as with my own Rough Riders, experience showed that the non-commissioned officers could usually carry on the fight by themselves if they were once started, no matter whether their officers were killed or not.

At this particular time it was trying for the men, as they were lying flat on their faces, very rarely responding to the bullets, shells, and shrapnel which swept over the hill-top, and which occasionally killed or wounded one of their number. Major Albert G. Forse, of the First Cavalry, a noted Indian fighter, was killed about this time. One of my best men, Sergeant Greenly, of Arizona, who was lying beside me, suddenly said, "Beg pardon,

Colonel; but I've been hit in the leg." I asked, "Badly?" He said, "Yes, Colonel; quite badly." After one of his comrades had helped him fix up his leg with a first-aid-to-the-injured bandage, he limped off to the rear.

None of the white regulars or Rough Riders showed the slightest sign of weakening; but under the strain the colored infantrymen (who had none of their officers) began to get a little uneasy and to drift to the rear, either helping wounded men, or saying that they wished to find their own regiments. This I could not allow, as it was depleting my line, so I jumped up, and walking a few yards to the rear, drew my revolver, halted the retreating soldiers, and called out to them that I appreciated the gallantry with which they had fought and would be sorry to hurt them, but that I should shoot the first man who, on any pretence whatever, went to the rear. My own men had all sat up and were watching my movements with the utmost interest. . . . I ended my statement to the colored soldiers by saying: "Now, I shall be very sorry to hurt you, and you don't know whether or not I will keep my word, but my men can tell you that I always do"; whereupon my cow-punchers, hunters, and miners solemnly nodded their heads and commented in chorus, exactly as if in a comic opera, "He always does; he always does!"

This was the end of the trouble, for the "smoked Yankees"—as the Spaniards called the colored soldiers—flashed their white teeth at one another, as they broke into broad grins, and I had no more trouble with them, they seeming to accept me as one of their own officers. The colored cavalrymen had already so accepted me; in return, the Rough Riders, although for the most part Southwesterners, who have a strong color prejudice, grew to accept them with hearty good-will as comrades, and were entirely willing, in their own phrase, "to drink out of the same canteen."

19

PRESLEY HOLLIDAY

Colored Officers or No Colored Soldiers
1900

After the declaration of war against Spain, thousands of African American men volunteered to serve in the military, motivated by hopes of freeing Cuba and obtaining equal rights at home through their demonstrated patriotism and service. Yet the military was a problematic vehicle for racial advancement, given that it was segregated at the time and that it excluded black men from most commissioned officer positions. Despite winning twenty-six Certificates of Merit and five Congressional Medals of Honor, black volunteers were welcomed home with less general acclaim than white soldiers were. In this selection, taken from a letter to the editor printed in the New York Age, *Sergeant Presley Holliday counters Roosevelt's aspersions on black soldiers. (See Document 18.)*

The Colonel [Roosevelt] made a slight error when he saw his mixed command contained some colored infantry. All the colored troops in that command were cavalrymen. His command consisted mostly of Rough Riders, with an aggregate of about one troop of the Tenth Cavalry, a few of the Ninth and a few of the First Regular Cavalry, with a half-dozen officers. Every few minutes brought men from the rear, everybody seeming to be anxious to get to the firing line. For a while we kept up a desultory fire, but as we could not locate the enemy (which all the time kept up a hot fire on our position), we became disgusted and lay down and kept silent. . . .

There were frequent calls for men to carry the wounded to the rear, to go for ammunition, and as night came on, to go for rations and entrenching tools. A few colored soldiers volunteered, as did some from the Rough Riders. It then happened that two men of the Tenth were ordered to the rear by Lieutenant Fleming, Tenth Cavalry, who was then

Presley Holliday, *New York Age*, May 11, 1899, as reprinted in Booker T. Washington, N. B. Wood, and Fannie Barrier Williams, *A New Negro for a New Century* (Chicago: American Publishing House, n.d.), 56–62.

present with part of his troop, for the purpose of bringing either rations or entrenching tools, and Colonel Roosevelt, seeing so many men going to the rear, shouted to them to come back, jumped up and drew his revolver, and told the men of the Tenth that he would shoot the first man who attempted to shirk duty by going to the rear, that he had orders to hold that line and he would do so if he had to shoot every man there to do it. His own men immediately informed him that "you won't have to shoot those men, Colonel. We know those boys." He was also assured by Lieutenant Flemming [*sic*] of the Tenth that he would have no trouble keeping them there, and some of our men shouted, in which I joined, that "we will stay with you, Colonel." Everyone who saw the incident knew the Colonel was mistaken about our men trying to shirk duty, but well knew that he could not admit of any heavy detail from his command, so no one thought ill of the matter. Inasmuch as the Colonel came to the line of the Tenth the next day and told the men of his threat to shoot some of their members and, as he expressed it, he had seen his mistake and found them to be far different men from what he supposed, I thought he was sufficiently conscious of his error not to make so ungrateful a statement about us at a time when the nation is about to recognize our past service. . . .

I could give many other incidents of our men's devotion to duty, of their determination to stay until the death, but what's the use? Colonel Roosevelt has said they shirked, and the reading public will take the Colonel at his word and go on thinking they shirked. His statement was uncalled for and uncharitable, and considering the moral and physical effect the advance of the Tenth Cavalry had in weakening the forces opposed to the Colonel's regiment both at Las Guasimas and San Juan Hill,[1] altogether ungrateful, and has done us an immeasurable lot of harm.

And, further, as to our lack of qualifications for command, I will say that when our soldiers who can and will write history sever their connections with the regular army and thus release themselves from their voluntary status of military lockjaw and tell what they saw, those who now preach that the negro is not fit to exercise command over troops and will go no further than he is led by [white] officers, will see in print held up for public gaze, much to their chagrin, tales of those Cuban battles that have never been told outside the tent and the barrack room, tales that it will not be agreeable to some of them to hear. The public will then learn that not every troop or company of colored soldiers who

[1] Battles on the march to Santiago.

took part in the assaults on San Juan Hill or El Caney[2] was led or urged forward by its white officer.

It is unfortunate that we had no colored officers in that campaign, and this thing of white officers for colored troops is exasperating, and I join with *The Age* in saying our motto for the future must be: "Colored officers or no colored soldiers."

[2]To reach Santiago, the U.S. Army launched a two-prong attack, with the left prong targeting San Juan Hill and Kettle Hill and the right prong, El Caney.

20

JOHN CLIFFORD BROWN

I Have Really Enjoyed the Hardships, the Excitement, the Change

1901

John Clifford Brown was one of some 125,000 U.S. soldiers who served in the Philippines from 1898 to 1902. A graduate of the Massachusetts Institute of Technology, he enlisted in the Army following the declaration of war against Spain. His regiment made it no farther than Camp Chickamauga, Georgia. In 1899, he reenlisted as a private in the Corps of Engineers. The Army sent him to the Philippines as a cartographer. He returned to the United States weighing less than 90 pounds after becoming disabled from typhoid fever. He died in January 1901. The bridge building that Brown refers to in this selection from his diary was part of a larger project of road construction for military purposes.

October 15[, 1899]. Heavy firing last night. I don't know where nor why. . . . I find my adjectives fail me when I try to describe the beauty and charm of this country. It is the garden spot of the world. That will have to cover it. I do not think the natives have any more heart in the fight. It is a common sight to see their officers beating them to make them stay

John Clifford Brown, *Diary of a Soldier in the Philippines* (Portland, Maine: privately printed, 1901), 81–82, 110, 148–49, 166, 218, 219, 223.

in the trenches. The Macabebes[1] are for us and are enlisting in as large numbers as can be allowed. After a fight I have an idea that they scatter to their homes and do not join the insurgents again unless forced to. As more and more territory passes into our hands the native army diminishes. Their ammunition is very short and poor. Most of their powder they make themselves. Not one-half of their army has rifles. . . .

November 20. Left Binalowen about 11 A.M. with Maj. Ballance's battalion of the 22d (A, F, L, K) and marched (I on pony) thirteen miles south, through Ornatuna to Vassalis,[2] arriving there 4:30 A.M. The battalion is living on the country and half the men have no shoes. No one in the army (Lawton's division) except the Cavalry have blankets or ponchos now. Road very bad, for miles is water waist deep and deep mud at intervals. Road lies through rice fields, which the natives are harvesting, with many small barrios or collections of huts. Drank the milk of green cocoanuts, which are six times as big as the ripe ones and hold about a quart of cool, fresh-tasting, colorless liquid. A very populous country. Natives seem glad to see us and bring us sugar and rice. . . .

November 21. I shall really be sorry if the insurrection is indeed ended. I have really enjoyed the hardships, the excitement, the change. I am convinced this is the healthiest climate in the world. We have been "hiked" about in mud and rain, sleeping on the ground without blankets, feet and clothes almost continually wet, and yet the men, notwithstanding short rations, are not sick. I do not think I have ever been in better health. . . .

January 7. . . . This native civilization is a curious thing. It does not seem able to stand alone. With the Spanish it rose to a certain height, just high enough to want to go further, but it can't do it alone. With America back of the government it will reach a high standard, but I am convinced that at no time will they ever be capable of really governing themselves. Even the educated Filipinos are childish. It seems to be their nature. I do not think time will ever change it any more than it has the nature of British India. I do not think any one will say they are capable of self-government. Am pleased that the sentiment in the States seems so overwhelmingly in favor of keeping the islands. . . .

March 10. Manila. Was made a Lance Corporal. "Lance Jack," we call it, duties and privileges of a corporal and pay of a private. Of course it's

---

[1] Filipinos from the town of Macabebe.
[2] Also spelled Binalonan, Urdaneta, and Villasis, these three towns are situated about one hundred miles north of Manila.

another step up and I am grateful. . . . I never will have to "walk post" again. I shall never "do fatigue." I am a boss. . . .

June 12. Paranaque.[3] The days are almost always overcast now, a welcome relief from the sun. It is curious, a curious sort of picture, to see us at work. There are four of us white men, only one of whom does any work. The rest of us sit round in the shade, under a native house perhaps with its hogs, children and perhaps a horse, and watch. The foreman has a native sweetheart who is usually squatting at his feet or following his movements with a dog-like devotion. They are mostly animal, these natives. It was only a couple of days ago that the President (a native) of Bacon, a town some ten miles from here, was caught alone and unarmed and cruelly butchered with bolos.[4]

June 13. Paranaque. Work on the bridge suspended temporarily for want of material. A lazy day in consequence. . . .

June 14. Another lazy day. No work on bridge as there was no lumber or stone. . . .

June 18. Rain all day. No work on the bridge, owing to lack of material. . . .

June 25. Paranaque. For the past week I have been trying to compare the negro with the Filipino. Now it may be objected, after the City of Para[5] and my experience here, that I am prejudiced against the negro. Well, possibly I am, but it is also certain that I waste no love on the Filipino, however much I admire his courtesy. Here I get a good chance to compare them. To the best of my belief if the Filipino had had the opportunity that the negro has had since the Civil War he would be a superior race mentally to our American negro. The negro is of course by long odds his superior physically. Now the two races are about on a par. I really cannot choose between them but I think the Filipino gives more promise for the future. It's a difficult question.

---

[3] A town several miles south of Manila.

[4] Machete-like knives.

[5] This is the name of the ship that transported Brown to the Philippines. He mentions African Americans twice in his account of the voyage. His August 5 entry notes that one of the colored infantry died on board and was buried unceremoniously at sea. His August 13 entry starts as follows: "Have been kept on the ship. The niggers left on the 11th and very glad we were to have them go."

21

G. E. MEYER

They Were Brandishing Bolos and Clubs and Yelling like Devils

1931

On September 28, 1901, Filipino insurgents attacked U.S. forces stationed in the town of Balangiga in the eastern Philippine island of Samar. The resulting slaughter—around fifty U.S. soldiers killed—was the worst loss of life suffered by the Americans in a single incident during the Philippine-American War, yet the Filipino toll that day was even higher, about 250 dead. The U.S. military later retaliated by killing almost the entire remaining population of the town. It then burned Balangiga to the ground in an action portending the scorched-earth tactics soon taken across Samar. A Ninth Infantry veteran named G .E. Meyer penned this account a number of years after the event. The looted church bells from Balangiga remain in U.S. military custody, despite requests for their return.

On August 11, 1901, we reached Balangiga. The town then contained about 1,000 inhabitants and consisted of the usual collection of thatched huts, called nipa shacks. The public buildings were, of course, a little more pretentious. We were welcomed by the Presidente, Chief of Police, and others, all professing great friendship. The Presidente and towns-people met us out in the harbor a mile from shore in small barotas and helped take our supplies ashore, giving the officers the convent adjoining the church to live in, and the Tribunal for fifty of the men's quarters, also two other nipa shacks for the remainder of the company. Every courtesy possible was shown us by them.

To one who has never been in the tropics, it is hard to picture the difficulties with which our troops had to contend subduing the insurgent Filipinos. The interior of Samar was a trackless jungle, cleft by immense mountain gorges. Deep and rapid streams, rugged, densely forested mountains, widespread morasses, and rice and mango swamps

---

G. E. Meyer, "The Massacre of Balangiga," in *The Massacre of Balangiga: Being an Authentic Account by Several of the Few Survivors*, ed. James O. Taylor (Joplin, Mo.: McCarn Printing Co., 1931), 2–6.

abounded. The natural wildness of the country, however, was but a part of our troubles. The enemy's spring traps and pitfalls with the sharp-pointed stakes at the bottom, cunningly covered over with earth and leaves, had to be guarded against. The intense heat of the tropical sun, fever, and the treacherous character of the natives added to our hard-ships. Often the insurgents would silently steal up on our men while on the march through the dense undergrowth, thrust their bolos through any soldier they caught unawares, and, quick as a flash, dart back into the thicket. This kind of fighting was nerve wracking, as the enemy could rarely be reached or even seen. From this, you may judge that ours was no bed of roses in the Philippines. But to return to Balangiga.

Our company had been in the town a few weeks when Captain Connell ordered the Presidente and Chief of Police to have each villager clear away the garbage and filth piled under his individual hut, in order to check the spread of cholera. The native shack rested upon four logs or trunks of trees standing upright, one at each corner, the floor being about six feet above the ground. The native climbed into the huts by means of bamboo ladders. On the ground beneath the flooring, the natives threw every kind of filth, and it was rarely one could approach a hut without holding his nose. The order was translated into Spanish and read and posted at every corner of each block by the Presidente.

This order, however, was not obeyed by the townspeople, so a second order was issued with the same results, and a third. The city staff, which consisted of a Presidente, a Catholic priest, and a police force of eight men, claimed that it was impossible to get the people to respond to the Captain's orders and asked for assistance. Accordingly, one day, about sundown, soon after retreat, the Captain turned out the company, sur-rounded the town, and brought in all men over eighteen years of age. We picked out eighty of the most able-bodied and held them prisoners, placing them in two conical tents, a few yards from the guardhouse, and placed a guard over them. The remainder of the townspeople were turned loose with the promise that they would return for work in the morning, which they did.

Each morning thereafter our sentinels would take about ten men each and start them cleaning up the streets, while the police staff saw that each family was cleaning up around their own nipa shacks. The natives were likewise assigned to clear away the underbrush, which grew thick in and around the town, as it might afford cover for an insurgent attack. Detachments of our soldiers also scouted the country in the vicinity. Captain Connell, however, was instructed to cultivate friendly relation-ship with the townspeople. They were to be allowed to keep possession of their houses, to go about their usual business, and to hold religious services in the town church without interference. . . .

On September 26th, the Chief of Police and the Presidente suggested to the Captain that, since Balangiga was the headquarters for the various surrounding towns, and since it was necessary for the natives to work out their taxes, they should be brought into Balangiga and be allowed to work it out there. The Captain thought this plan quite reasonable and agreed. The Chief of Police accordingly went out into the mountains and brought back forty strong, husky men. We turned forty of the town prisoners loose, placed these men in the tents, and made the townspeople promise to return in the morning for work, which they did. The next day the Chief went out and got forty more men, put them in the other tent and let the rest of the townspeople loose with the same promise. These eighty prisoners, brought in by the Chief, were not tax workers, but eighty of General Lukban's[1] trained bolomen. . . .

On the morning of September 28th, I was musician of the guard, and sounded the mess call for our men, who prepared for breakfast. We were compelled to carry our guns loaded at all times, except at mess table. If ten of us went out bathing, five remained on shore to guard. The mess table for barracks Nos. 5 and 3 was next to the kitchen, two rods from the main barracks, and ours was under our shack. We never doubted that however strong the attack we would have time to reach our rifles. About midnight Private Gamlin reported to the Sergeant of the Guard that he thought the women and children were leaving town. Many prayers were heard during the night by the same guard, but he thought they were preparing for another earthquake and gave it no further attention.

At six-thirty the natives were gathering for the day's work. Many were lounging around the plaza, bolo in hand. The prisoners were grouped near the tents within a few feet of a pile of bolos, picks and shovels. Nearly all of our men were in the mess tent eating breakfast. I, with Corporal Burke and about twelve messmates, had just sat down in front of Post No. 3 and were about to eat. Looking around, I noticed the Chief of Police accompanied by some of his followers walk from Post No. 2 to Post No. 3 where a sentinel was stationed. As the sentinel passed him, the Chief of Police suddenly snatched the rifle out of his hands, knocked him senseless with the butt and yelled, firing at the same time into our group and wounding one of the men. The natives who were hidden

---

[1] General Vicente Lukban headed Filipino forces in Samar.

in the church rushed in and killed the officers and guard; the prisoners rushed out, grabbing their working bolos, and guarded the doors
of the main barracks, slashing down every man who ventured along.
There was a succession of shouts, the tower bells rang out a deafening
appeal, and the crowd of natives headed by the Chief of Police rushed
toward us with the evident intention of cutting us off from our weapons
in the barracks. They were brandishing bolos and clubs and yelling like
devils.

22

EDWARD J. DAVIS

They Held Him under the Faucet

1902

*Edward J. Davis was called on to testify about the "water cure" as part of
an investigation into U.S. military conduct in the Philippines. Reports of
U.S. military misdeeds—including burning villages and killing prisoners—had trickled out of the Philippines from early in the war, despite
military censorship. Anti-imperialist calls for an investigation resulted in
congressional hearings in 1902. But rather than falling under the aegis
of an independent committee, the hearings came under the authority of the
Committee on the Philippines, headed by Republican senator Henry Cabot
Lodge. An arch supporter of U.S. policies in the Philippines, Lodge worked
to turn the hearings into a vindication of the administration's policies and
the U.S. military's conduct of the war. Yet over the ten weeks of testimony,
stories of "cruelties" also made it into the official record.*

Q. Mr. Davis, when did you enlist in the Army?—A. I enlisted the
15th of July, 1899.
Q. What time did you arrive in the Philippines?—A. October 3, 1899. . . .

Testimony of Edward J. Davis, *Affairs in the Philippine Islands: Hearings before the Committee on the Philippines of the United States Senate*, 57th Cong., 1st Sess., doc. 331, part 2
(Washington, D.C.: Government Printing Office, 1902), 1726–28.

Q. When did you first arrive at Igbaras?[1]—A. I had charge of that detachment at Igbaras; I do not remember the date I went over there. I was in Igbaras myself about seven months, and I had charge of the detachment there, a detachment of 15 men. . . .

Q. Who were the officers in command?—A. Captain Glenn was in command, Lieutenant Conger was in command of the scouts, and Dr. Lyons was there; he was the contract surgeon.

Q. What time did they arrive?—A. It was just daybreak.

Q. On what day?—A. I could not tell you the day.

Q. They arrived about daybreak?—A. Yes, sir.

Q. Was it about the 27th of November, 1900?—A. Yes, sir; it was somewhere about that.

Q. You may state whether or not the president or mayor of Igbaras was taken into custody that day.—A. He was.

Q. And where was he brought?—A. He was brought to the convent. I went for him myself.

Q. By whose order was he arrested?—A. Orders from Captain Glenn.

Q. Where did you take him?—A. I took him to the convent.

Q. After he arrived there about what time in the morning was it?—A. It was about 7 o'clock, I should judge.

Q. After he was taken there what was done with him?—A. He was taken out into a big hall in the convent there, his clothes were all taken off, his hands were tied behind him, and he was asked for information in regard to runners being sent up into the mountains; asked if the scouts had arrived there. He would not give this information, so they took him to this water tank. It was a tank holding about a hundred gallons of water. They held him under the faucet and he was made to take this water into his mouth at the command of Captain Glenn. . . .

Q. How was his mouth kept open?—A. It was kept open with a stick, but I can not describe just how the stick was, because they had their hands over his mouth most of the time.

Q. And after he was filled up with water, what else was done with him?—A. After they filled him up with water he swelled way up and then these two soldiers would roll the water out of him. They had an interpreter over him and they asked him if he would tell what information they were after. He told some, and then after they released him and he had walked away and they were going out in the mountains somewhere, and they got downstairs, they wanted further information out of him in regard to these runners going out into the mountains,

[1] A pueblo on Panay Island, near the center of the Philippine archipelago.

and he would not give it. So they took him down right there and they
took a syringe and squirted water up his nostrils. He would not give
the information then and they put salt in the water. Then he was willing to tell. . . .

Q. About how long was this continued, how long was he kept bound?—
A. When he was under the tank of water he was kept there as much
as five or ten minutes. They filled him clear up, and it would swell his
stomach until all through here would be good and hard [indicating],
and then they would roll him, would roll the water out of him.

Q. What was that process?—A. They took their fists like that [indicating].

Q. On his stomach?—A. Yes, sir.

Q. His body was not rolled over?—A. No, sir.

Q. But they would double up their fists in the way you indicated?—
A. Yes, they would double up their fists and water would squirt out
of his mouth.

Q. What, if any, manifestations of pain did he show?—A. He screeched
terribly, and his eyes were all bloodshot, from, I suppose, taking the
water.

23

CARLOS P. ROMULO

I Hated Those Blue-Eyed Foreign Devils
1961

*Carlos P. Romulo was a Philippine author, diplomat, and soldier who served
as president of the UN General Assembly from 1949 to 1950. Romulo wrote
this account during the Cold War, when the independent Philippines was
a U.S. ally. Romulo's father was not alone in choosing to work with his
former opponents. Many Filipino nationalists eventually joined forces with
the U.S. occupiers to advance their own economic and political power. Significantly, the revolutionary government had been elitist from the start: Its
congressional delegates were overwhelmingly landowners, merchants, and*

professionals, and its suffrage provisions were highly exclusionary. Many members of this resilient oligarchy went on to collaborate with the Japanese regime during World War II and then to repudiate Japanese rule in 1945.

I remember, as distinctly as if I were that child again, lying in my bed at night and hearing the creak of the kitchen door and my mother and father whispering together. Then I knew my anonymous soldier-father had crept into his home again after days spent fighting the American soldiers in our hills.

My hearing was as acute as my memory. My parents never knew how much I learned from their whisperings.

I learned to fear for my father's life and the presence of his enemies. I learned who they were. They were the "bad men," the American soldiers who were bivouacked in the Plaza, not four blocks away from our home.

I hated those blue-eyed foreign devils, with a child's helpless hatred.

I would hear my father's final whisper to my mother, "Don't let the boys go near the Plaza."

So of course I had to go there.

As one probes an aching tooth, so I found myself drawn to the little park where the enemy sat around their camp-fires, cleaning the guns that might any day take my father's life from us; cooking, eating, joking, singing, as if they were men and not monsters. They sang sad lonely songs for their homeland, and although I did not know the meaning of the words their sadness almost melted my heart. . . .

They seemed as unhappy at finding themselves strangers in a strange land as we were at having them here.

But they had other, hateful songs, and while I could not understand these either I knew they were tuneful insults to my people. Some of these intruders in our country were quite obviously looking down on the Filipinos as members of an inferior race.

It was my first suspicion of race hatred and I found it difficult to bear. How dared the crude, rough-speaking strangers look down on us!

I would return to a household gentled by centuries of civilized living, and curl up in a comfortable chair to puzzle my way through this mystery. I reached the conclusion that these Americans, who represented the America I hated, dared look down on my parents and their good, sober, industrious neighbors, and label them outlaws, simply because we were not free.

Because the Philippines was not a free country children were taught to smuggle food and ammunition to their fathers hiding in the woods; wives met their husbands under cover of darkness, good men hid in the hills and crept home by stealth, like guilty animals; and women stood by their doors in icy contempt while American soldiers violated the privacy of their homes searching for men and guns.

All this—because we were not free.

Then . . . two terrible events happened in rapid succession. I went to the Plaza one morning and found the body of our neighbor Clemente hanging on the gallows the Americans had built in our little park. He was a good family man and the father of several of my playmates. Shortly after I learned from a whispered midnight conversation between my parents that my good, kind grandfather, the head of our family, had been captured by American soldiers and given the "water cure" when he refused to tell where my father was hiding.

I had no idea what the water cure was, and it was years before I learned it was a form of torture revived by these twentieth-century American soldiers from the Spanish Inquisition. Water was forced into the victim's stomach by means of a funnel or tube, so that the tortured one sometimes ruptured, often died.

By the time I learned this I also had learned that such acts in the Philippines were limited to a few sadistic soldiers of the type that can be found in any army or any neighborhood. But when I was three I had no such facts to comfort me. I blamed America and our not being free.

My grandfather came back to us, somehow older and gentler and saddened, and he did not live very long after that. What had been done to him was never discussed before the children and I could not tell anyone that I knew. Since I could not talk the matter out it festered in my mind and added to the fear I felt for my father and to my hatred of the Americans.

Why did these horrors serve to draw me back to the Plaza?

Wide-eyed and wondering I watched the soldiers eating and singing around their campfires, and in my innocence wondered why God did not strike them dead.

Then, as I have told so many times . . . an American sergeant whose name I never knew lured a half-dozen small Filipino youngsters to his side. He gave us the American fruit we had never tasted—apples—and read to us from a wonderful little book called Baldwin's *Primer*. Did he have small boys at home and was he lonely for them?

This must have been the truth of it, for he and other soldiers drew us against our will into their adult military circle. They knew how small boys love to be treated—as men among men. Soon we were on a comradely basis, and since they could not speak our language it seemed natural that we should learn theirs. . . .

I came to trust our enemies, to love them, and knew at last there was no difference between us, because we were friends.

In this I did not feel disloyal to my father and his cause. Friendship was a personal matter. It had nothing to do with war. It had no effect on my hatred for America. . . .

The year 1902 saw final surrender, but the Filipino dream of freedom did not surrender. For the Filipinos had been promised eventual freedom by America, so all would be well.

My father was a leader of popular opinion in our town. He was fairminded and temperate. He argued that since America had beaten us and then made its generous promise, the only honorable attitude for the Filipinos to take was to cooperate fully. He was among the last in our town to surrender and to take the oath of allegiance to the United States. But he was the first man in Camiling to learn English. In time he became a teacher of English. He made friends with the American schoolteachers who came to our country and one of them, an American major, became such a close friend that he came to live with us in our home and was a sort of extra uncle to us children.

My father began the study of civic welfare that was ultimately to lead him into a political career. He studied the American form of government and became a leader in the fair government campaigns. He sought to see the good in all that the Americans were doing to help advance the Filipinos—new schools, better roads, medical and hygienic care. He praised these works and pointed out their advantages to his own people. He became the advocate in our province for the American way. . . .

For despite defeat my father's head was still high. By his willingness to see the merits in and cooperate with the new form of government he was developing into a leader who in the long run would guide his fellow patriots back to freedom.

5

The Case for Taking and Holding the Philippines

24

WILLIAM MCKINLEY

Doing Our Duty by Them

1899

President William McKinley was elected to his first term as president in 1896, on the Republican ticket. Having been criticized for his hesitancy to ask Congress to declare war against Spain, he ran for reelection as a successful war president, with the famous veteran of the Cuban campaign, Theodore Roosevelt, as his running mate. McKinley was assassinated shortly after the start of his second term, in 1901. This is one of a series of speeches that he delivered to build support for his administration's policies in the Philippines. His allusions to duty resonate with references to the "white man's burden." (See Document 3.)

We hear no complaint of the relations created by the war between this government and the islands of Cuba and Porto Rico. There are some, however, who regard the Philippines as in a different relation; but whatever variety of views there may be on this phase of the question, there is universal agreement that the Philippines shall not be turned back to Spain. [Great applause.] No true American consents to that. Even if unwilling to accept them ourselves, it would have been a weak evasion

---

William McKinley, "Speech at Dinner of the Home Market Club, Boston, February 16, 1899," in *Speeches and Addresses of William McKinley, from March 1, 1897 to May 30, 1900* (New York: Doubleday and McClure, 1900), 187–93.

of duty to require Spain to transfer them to some other power or powers, and thus shirk our own responsibility. Even if we had had, as we did not have, the power to compel such a transfer, it could not have been made without the most serious international complications. Such a course could not be thought of. And yet, had we refused to accept the cession of them, we should have had no power over them, even for their own good. . . . The other suggestions—first, that they should be tossed into the arena of contention for the strife of nations; or, second, be left to the anarchy and chaos of no protectorate at all—were too shameful to be considered. The treaty gave them to the United States. Could we have required less and done our duty? [Cries of "No!"] Could we, after freeing the Filipinos from the domination of Spain, have left them without government and without power to protect life or property or to perform the international obligations essential to an independent state? Could we have left them in a state of anarchy and justified ourselves in our own consciences or before the tribunal of mankind? Could we have done that in the sight of God or man?

Our concern was not for territory or trade or empire, but for the people whose interests and destiny, without our willing it, had been put in our hands. [Great applause.] It was with this feeling that, from the first day to the last, not one word or line went from the Executive in Washington to our military and naval commanders at Manila, or to our peace commissioners at Paris, that did not put as the sole purpose to be kept in mind, first after the success of our arms and the maintenance of our own honor, the welfare and happiness and the rights of the inhabitants of the Philippine Islands. [Great and long-continued applause.] Did we need their consent to perform a great act for humanity? We had it in every aspiration of their minds, in every hope of their hearts. Was it necessary to ask their consent to capture Manila, the capital of their islands? [Laughter.] Did we ask their consent to liberate them from Spanish sovereignty, or to enter Manila Bay and destroy the Spanish sea-power there? We did not ask these things; we were obeying a higher moral obligation which rested on us and which did not require anybody's consent. [Great applause and cheering.] We were doing our duty by them, as God gave us the light to see our duty, with the consent of our own consciences and with the approval of civilization. [Applause.] Every present obligation has been met and fulfilled in the expulsion of Spanish sovereignty from their islands and while the war that destroyed it was in progress we could not ask their views. Nor can we now ask their consent. Indeed, can any one tell me in what form it could be marshaled and ascertained until peace and order, so necessary to the reign of reason, shall be secured and established? [Applause.] A reign of terror is not the kind of rule under which right action and deliberate judgment are possible. It is not a good time for the liberator to submit important questions concerning liberty and government to the liberated while they are engaged in shooting down their rescuers. [Applause and cheering.] . . .

Until Congress shall direct otherwise, it will be the duty of the Executive to possess and hold the Philippines, giving to the people thereof peace and order and beneficent government; affording them every opportunity to prosecute their lawful pursuits; encouraging them in thrift and industry; making them feel and know that we are their friends, not their enemies, that their good is our aim, that their welfare is our welfare, but that neither their aspirations nor ours can be realized until our authority is acknowledged and unquestioned. [Loud and enthusiastic applause.]

That the inhabitants of the Philippines will be benefited by this republic is my unshaken belief. That they will have a kindlier government under our guidance, and that they will be aided in every possible way to be a self-respecting and self-governing people, is as true as that the American people love liberty and have an abiding faith in their own government and in their own institutions. [Great applause.] No imperial designs lurk in the American mind. They are alien to American sentiment, thought, and purpose. Our priceless principles undergo no change under a tropical sun. They go with the flag. [Long continued applause.]

25

THEODORE ROOSEVELT

The Man Must Be Glad to Do a Man's Work

1899

Having suffered acutely from asthma as a child, Theodore Roosevelt toughened his body through strenuous pursuits such as hunting and ranching in the Dakotas. Though ridiculed as an effeminate dude when he first ran for the New York Assembly, his military service in

Theodore Roosevelt, "The Strenuous Life," in *American Ideals, the Strenuous Life, Realizable Ideals*, ed. Hermann Hagedorn (New York: Charles Scribner's Sons, 1926), 319–23.

Cuba helped him present himself to the U.S. public as a hardened warrior. When he ran successfully for governor of New York in 1898, he campaigned as a paragon of military masculinity with Rough Riders at his side. Wanting a war hero on the ballot, President William McKinley chose Roosevelt as his vice presidential running mate for the 1900 election. Roosevelt delivered this speech to the wealthy members of Chicago's all-male Hamilton Club.

In speaking to you, men of the greatest city of the West, men of the State which gave to the country Lincoln and Grant, men who preeminently and distinctly embody all that is most American in the American character, I wish to preach, not the doctrine of ignoble ease, but the doctrine of the strenuous life, the life of toil and effort, of labor and strife; to preach that highest form of success which comes, not to the man who desires mere easy peace, but to the man who does not shrink from danger, from hardship, or from bitter toil, and who out of these wins the splendid ultimate triumph.

A life of slothful ease, a life of that peace which springs merely from lack either of desire or of power to strive after great things, is as little worthy of a nation as of an individual. I ask only that what every self-respecting American demands from himself and from his sons shall be demanded of the American nation as a whole. Who among you would teach your boys that ease, that peace, is to be the first consideration in their eyes—to be the ultimate goal after which they strive? You men of Chicago have made this city great, you men of Illinois have done your share, and more than your share, in making America great, because you neither preach nor practise such a doctrine. If you are rich and are worth your salt, you will teach your sons that though they may have leisure, it is not to be spent in idleness; for wisely used leisure merely means that those who possess it, being free from the necessity of working for their livelihood, are all the more bound to carry on some kind of non-remunerative work in science, in letters, in art, in exploration, in historical research—work of the type we most need in this country, the successful carrying out of which reflects most honor upon the nation. We do not admire the man of timid peace. We admire the man who embodies victorious effort; the man who never wrongs his neighbor, who is prompt to help a friend, but who has those virile qualities necessary to win in the strife of actual life. It is hard to fail, but it is worse never to have tried to succeed. . . .

In the last analysis a healthy state can exist only when the men and women who make it up lead clean, vigorous, healthy lives; when the children are so trained that they shall endeavor, not to shirk difficulties, but to overcome them; not to seek ease, but to know how to wrest triumph from toil and risk. The man must be glad to do a man's work, to dare and endure and to labor; to keep himself, and to keep those dependent upon him. The woman must be the housewife, the helpmeet of the homemaker, the wise and fearless mother of many healthy children. . . . When men fear work or fear righteous war, when women fear motherhood, they tremble on the brink of doom; and well it is that they should vanish from the earth, where they are fit subjects for the scorn of all men and women who are themselves strong and brave and high-minded.

As it is with the individual, so it is with the nation. It is a base untruth to say that happy is the nation that has no history. Thrice happy is the nation that has a glorious history. Far better it is to dare mighty things, to win glorious triumphs, even though checkered by failure, than to take rank with those poor spirits who neither enjoy much nor suffer much, because they live in the gray twilight that knows not victory nor defeat. If in 1861 the men who loved the Union had believed that peace was the end of all things, and war and strife the worst of all things, and had acted up to their belief, we would have saved hundreds of thousands of lives, we would have saved hundreds of millions of dollars. Moreover, besides saving all the blood and treasure we then lavished, we would have prevented the heartbreak of many women, the dissolution of many homes, and we would have spared the country those months of gloom and shame when it seemed as if our armies marched only to defeat. We could have avoided all this suffering simply by shrinking from strife. And if we had thus avoided it, we would have shown that we were weaklings, and that we were unfit to stand among the great nations of the earth. Thank God for the iron in the blood of our fathers, the men who upheld the wisdom of Lincoln, and bore sword or rifle in the armies of Grant! Let us, the children of the men who proved themselves equal to the mighty days, let us, the children of the men who carried the great Civil War to a triumphant conclusion, praise the God of our fathers that the ignoble counsels of peace were rejected; that the suffering and loss, the blackness of sorrow and despair, were unflinchingly faced, and the years of strife endured; for in the end the slave was freed, the Union restored, and the mighty American republic placed once more as a helmeted queen among nations.

We of this generation do not have to face a task such as that our fathers faced, but we have our tasks, and woe to us if we fail to perform them!

We cannot, if we would, play the part of China,[1] and be content to rot by inches in ignoble ease within our borders, taking no interest in what goes on beyond them, sunk in a scrambling commercialism; heedless of the higher life, the life of aspiration, of toil and risk, busying ourselves only with the wants of our bodies for the day, until suddenly we should find, beyond a shadow of question, what China has already found, that in this world the nation that has trained itself to a career of unwarlike and isolated ease is bound, in the end, to go down before other nations which have not lost the manly and adventurous qualities. If we are to be a really great people, we must strive in good faith to play a great part in the world. We cannot avoid meeting great issues. All that we can determine for ourselves is whether we shall meet them well or ill. In 1898 we could not help being brought face to face with the problem of war with Spain. All we could decide was whether we should shrink like cowards from the contest, or enter into it as beseemed a brave and high-spirited people; and, once in, whether failure or success should crown our banners. So it is now. We cannot avoid the responsibilities that confront us in Hawaii, Cuba, Porto Rico, and the Philippines. All we can decide is whether we shall meet them in a way that will redound to the national credit, or whether we shall make of our dealings with these new problems a dark and shameful page in our history. To refuse to deal with them at all merely amounts to dealing with them badly. We have a given problem to solve. If we undertake the solution, there is, of course, always danger that we may not solve it aright; but to refuse to undertake the solution simply renders it certain that we cannot possibly solve it aright. The timid man, the lazy man, the man who distrusts his country, the over-civilized man, who has lost the great fighting, masterful virtues, the ignorant man, and the man of dull mind, whose soul is incapable of feeling the mighty life that thrills "stern men with empires in their brains"—all these, of course, shrink from seeing the nation undertake its new duties; shrink from seeing us build a navy and an army adequate to our needs; shrink from seeing us do our share of the world's work, by bringing order out of chaos in the great, fair tropic islands from which the valor of our soldiers and sailors has driven the Spanish flag. These are the men who fear the strenuous life, who fear the only national life which is really worth leading.

---

[1]After peaking around 1800, the Qing (also known as Manchu) dynasty declined over the nineteenth century, plagued by internal unrest and foreign attacks.

26

ALBERT J. BEVERIDGE

The Pacific Is Our Ocean

1900

Senator Albert J. Beveridge, a Republican from Indiana, was a lead-
ing advocate of imperialist policies in the Philippines. In debates over
Philippine policy, he had the rare advantage of firsthand experience in
the islands, due to a six-month trip he made in 1899. In response to
Beveridge's claims, opponents pointed out that holding the Philippines
would cost about $67.5 million a year and that, in a time of war with
an outside power, additional resources would be necessary for the col-
ony's defense. (See Document 30.)

The Philippines are ours forever, "territory belonging to the United
States," as the Constitution calls them. And just beyond the Philippines
are China's illimitable markets. We will not retreat from either. We will
not repudiate our duty in the archipelago. We will not abandon our opportunity in the Orient. We will not renounce our past in the mission of race,
trustee, under God, of the civilization of the world. And we will move
forward to our work, not howling out regrets like slaves whipped to their
burdens but with gratitude for a task worthy of our strength and thanks-
giving to Almighty God that He has marked us as His chosen people,
henceforth to lead in the regeneration of the world.

This island empire is the last land left in all the oceans. If it should
prove a mistake to abandon it, the blunder once made would be irre-
trievable. If it proves a mistake to hold it, the error can be corrected
when we will. Every other progressive nation stands ready to believe us.

But to hold it will be no mistake. Our largest trade henceforth must
be with Asia. The Pacific is our ocean. More and more Europe will man-
ufacture the most it needs, secure from its colonies the most it con-
sumes. Where shall we turn for consumers of our surplus? Geography
answers the question. China is our natural customer. She is nearer to us

---

Albert J. Beveridge, Senate Remarks, January 9, 1900, *Congressional Record*, 56th Cong.,
1st Sess., 704–12.

than to England, Germany, or Russia, the commercial powers of the present and the future. They have moved nearer to China by securing permanent bases on her borders. The Philippines give us a base at the door of all the East.

Lines of navigation from our ports to the Orient and Australia, from the Isthmian Canal to Asia, from all Oriental ports to Australia converge at and separate from the Philippines. They are a self-supporting, dividend-paying fleet, permanently anchored at a spot selected by the strategy of Providence, commanding the Pacific. And the Pacific is the ocean of the commerce of the future. Most future wars will be conflicts for commerce. The power that rules the Pacific, therefore, is the power that rules the world. And, with the Philippines, that power is and will forever be the American Republic.

China's trade is the mightiest commercial fact in our future. Her foreign commerce was $235,738,300 in 1897, of which we, her neighbor, had less than 9 per cent, of which only a little more than half was merchandise sold to China by us. We ought to have 50 per cent, and we will. And China's foreign commerce is only beginning. Her resources, her possibilities, her wants, all are undeveloped. She has only 340 miles of railway. I have seen trains loaded with natives and all the activities of modern life already appearing along the line. But she needs, and in fifty years will have, 20,000 miles of railway.

Who can estimate her commerce, then? That statesman commits a crime against American trade—against the American grower of cotton and wheat and tobacco, the American manufacturer of machinery and clothing—who fails to put America where she may command that trade. . . .

But if they did not command China, India, the Orient, the whole Pacific for purposes of offense, defense, and trade, the Philippines are so valuable in themselves that we should hold them. I have cruised more than 2,000 miles through the archipelago, every moment a surprise at its loveliness and wealth. I have ridden hundreds of miles on the islands, every foot of the way a revelation of vegetable and mineral riches.

No land in America surpasses in fertility the plains and valleys of Luzon. Rice and coffee, sugar and cocoanuts, hemp and tobacco, and many products of the temperate as well as the tropic zone grow in various sections of the archipelago. I have seen hundreds of bushels of Indian corn lying in a road fringed with banana trees. The forests of Negros, Mindanao, Mindora, Paluau, and parts of Luzon are invaluable and intact. The wood of the Philippines can supply the furniture of the world for a century to come. At Cebu the best informed man in the island told me that 40 miles of Cebu's mountain chain are practically mountains of coal. . . .

I have a nugget of pure gold picked up in its present form on the banks of a Philippine creek. I have gold dust washed out by crude processes of careless natives from the sands of a Philippine stream. Both indicate great deposits at the source from which they come. In one of the islands great deposits of copper exist untouched. The mineral wealth of this empire of the ocean will one day surprise the world. I base this statement partly on personal observation, but chiefly on the testimony of foreign merchants in the Philippines, who have practically investigated the subject, and upon the unanimous opinion of natives and priests. And the mineral wealth is but a small fraction of the agricultural wealth of these islands. . . .

Mr. President, this question is deeper than any question of party politics; deeper than any question of the isolated policy of our country even; deeper even than any question of constitutional power. It is elemental. It is racial. God has not been preparing the English-speaking and Teutonic peoples for a thousand years for nothing but vain and idle self-contemplation and self-admiration. No! He has given us the spirit of progress to overwhelm the forces of reaction throughout the earth. He has made us adepts in government that we may administer government among savage and senile peoples. Were it not for such a force as this the world would relapse into barbarism and night. And of all our race He has marked the American people as His chosen nation to finally lead in the regeneration of the world. This is the divine mission of America, and it holds for us all the profit, all the glory, all the happiness possible to man.

27

WILLIAM HOWARD TAFT

The Philippines for the Filipinos

1915

William Howard Taft became the first civilian governor general of the Philippines following his service as president of the Second Philippine Commission, formed in 1901 to shift the Philippines to civilian rule. After leaving the Philippines, Taft served as secretary of war and president of the United States (1909–1913), in which capacities he continued to insist that the Filipinos needed more U.S. tutelage before they were ready for self-government.

The work of the fifteen years, from the Treaty of Paris[1] until the incoming of the present administration, is something of which the American people have a right to be proud. We had had little or no experience in colonial government. We took over a people of whom 90 per cent were illiterate, utterly without training in self-government, with agriculture their only livelihood, ruined by the war and the anarchy and vandalism that followed, with diseases of men and draft cattle rampant in the islands. Slowly and with difficulty we constructed a government, with a civil service of Americans in control and Filipinos in subordinate places. We gave as much of local self-government in the municipalities and provinces as the people could safely exercise. We established courts and justice in all parts of the islands. With the United States Army first, and then with a native constabulary alone, we gave peace to the islands and opportunity for the arts of peace. We promoted the health of the islands by the application of the most modern methods of governmental hygiene regulation, quarantine and hospital service. By the construction of a most expensive road, we opened up within one hundred fifty

---

[1]Along with ending the war between the United States and Spain, the treaty transferred the Philippines to the United States for $20 million.

William Howard Taft, "Duty of the United States toward the Philippines," *Transactions* 10 (September 1915): 409–22; reprinted in *Selected Articles on Independence for the Philippines*, compiled by Julia E. Johnsen (New York: H. W. Wilson, 1921), 35–37.

miles, and half a day's railroad and automobile ride, of Manila, a beautiful mountain country with the climate and invigorating air of the temperate zone, five thousand feet above the sea, where hospitals, rest houses, schools, camps and hotels offer to the Filipino people an opportunity for recuperation from the depressing and enervating effects of the climate of their lowlands, — an opportunity which under American enterprise, the Filipino people are improving.

We introduced and perfected an educational system in which seven thousand Filipino teachers are giving near half a million of the children of school age in the islands a primary education in English, and added thereto industrial, high school and university facilities for those who could improve them.

We have granted the Filipinos the benefits of the free markets of the United States for their sugar, tobacco, copra[2] and hemp. We rid them of the political incubus and disturbing effect of the holding by monastic orders as landlords of four million acres of the best agricultural lands in the most populated districts of the islands, through governmental purchase. We stimulated the building of railroads and the great betterment of inter-island navigation. We promoted an extended system of highways in the islands, where there were but pony trails before, and aroused in the people a spirit of emulation in their construction and repair which has made greatly for ease of inter-communication between towns and provinces, and, of course, promoted commerce and the spread of intelligence. We readjusted the system of taxation off the poorer classes where it had rested in Spanish days, and gave the wealthier a fairer share of the burden. We made the administration of the tax laws uniform, honest, economical and productive, where it had been unequal, corrupt, wasteful and unproductive. In 1907 we created a popular assembly and made it a part of the legislative branch of the Philippine government. We retained a majority of Americans in the coordinate branch of the legislature called the Commission. We provided that if the Philippine Assembly refused to appropriate funds to support the Government, the appropriations of the previous year should be regarded as repeated and the same amount of funds be subject to executive warrant.

We found at first little sympathy in our novel colonial venture from the colonial authorities of those countries long engaged in colonial responsibilities, because of our announced purpose to educate the Filipino by a widespread English school system, and by a gradual extension of autonomy and the political education which it would slowly impart. But

[2]Dried coconut.

with the slogan of "the Philippines for the Filipinos" we pressed on, with Americans in ultimate control and guidance, and with Filipinos in all the places consistent with effective and progressive government.

The illiteracy of the great body of the Filipinos, the utter lack of political experience in the large sense of the small body of educated Filipinos, their entire lack of real understanding of a democratic constitutional government, and of the necessity for guarding individual rights and those of a minority, make the political education of the people slow. It will certainly need as long a time to train them in self-government as it will to educate all the people in primary branches of knowledge, and that will require at least two generations and perhaps more.

6

Objections to U.S. Philippine Policy

28

FELIPE AGONCILLO

The Right of the Filipinos to Their Self-Government

1899

Felipe Agoncillo served as the first chairman of the Filipino Revolutionary Committee. In the fall of 1898, he traveled to the United States as the representative of the Philippine Republic. President McKinley refused to recognize Agoncillo as an official representative, but he did meet with him as a private citizen. After reminding McKinley that the Filipinos had allied themselves with the United States in the war against Spain, Agoncillo pressed for a seat at the Paris peace conference and recognition of Philippine sovereignty. McKinley advised Agoncillo to make his case to the U.S. peace commissioners in Paris. Agoncillo traveled to Paris, but to no avail. The negotiators refused to meet with him and drafted a treaty with no provisions for Philippine independence.

In the struggle upon which the Filipinos have been engaged for . . . nearly a hundred years, they have been largely influenced and controlled in their hopes, aspirations and actions by the Declaration of Independence of the American people, particularly in so far as that document has declared that "all men are created equal, that they are endowed by

Felipe Agoncillo, "Memorandum Relative to the Right of the Philippine Republic to Recognition: Accompanying Letter to the Honorable the Secretary of State, of date January 11, 1899," pamphlet, 1–10.

their Creator with certain inalienable rights, that among these are life, liberty and the pursuit of happiness." They have further learned from the same document in their studies of American law and liberty that "to secure these rights, governments are instituted among men, deriving their just powers from the consent of the governed." They understand from it that colonial government is, as the Declaration of Independence says, "destructive of these ends," and that it is, therefore, the right of the people to "alter or abolish it, and to institute new government, laying its foundation on such principles and organizing its powers in such form as to them shall seem most likely to effect their safety and happiness." Further studying that instrument, they have found that it indicted the King of England for keeping among the Americans "in time of peace, standing armies, without the consent of (their) legislatures," and because he had "affected to render the military independent of, and superior to, the civil power." They have, therefore, also learned to be jealous of armies of any nationality, the presence of which might curtail their civil liberties, without their consent.

Finding themselves, therefore, subject to all the grievances as to government without representation, unjust taxation, quartering of military among them, subordination of civil to military power, they rose repeatedly in rebellion, and finally on the 18th of June last, being in possession at that time of the larger share of the Philippine Islands, the Spanish government being recognized even then over a comparatively small area, they formed an independent government. In the formation of this government and the drafting of its constitution, they provided for and insured to the independent people of the Philippine Islands the ends contemplated by the Constitution of the United States, establishing justice, insuring domestic tranquility, providing for the common defence, promoting the general welfare, and securing the blessings of liberty to them and their posterity.

At the time of the formation of this Constitution, parallel as it was practically in connection with their revolution to time of the adoption of the American Declaration of Independence, they found themselves superior in position as to their control over their country to that of the Americans, when the Declaration of Independence was framed; for the Spaniards possessed only a small portion of the islands, while the Filipinos were in control of nearly all of their large cities, as well as of the country beyond.

Acting under this constitution, they have carried out all of its injunctions, establishing justice, raising armies, maintaining a post-office system, and exercising the further legitimate functions of a government.

Their position at the present time is better, I respectfully suggest, so far as general recognition of their national authority is concerned, than was that of the American Republic prior to the ratification of a treaty between America and England; for, as you will recall, British armies were in possession of American ports when the treaty of peace was signed, whereas now, the Spanish government is recognized nowhere in the Philippine Islands, except part of the island of Mindanao; the Philippine Government reigning supreme everywhere, save at the City of Manila, and the town of Cavite, adjoining it. . . .

Recognizing, as the Americans have in their Declaration of Independence, in their constitution, and in their history of more than one hundred years, the absolute right of all nations to rule themselves, free from the control of alien masters, I submit to you, with entire confidence, the right of the Filipinos to their self-government.

29

[JULIUS F. TAYLOR]

They All Breathe an Utter Contempt
"for the Niggers"

1899

Although the African American press had generally supported U.S. intervention in the Spanish-Cuban War, due to sympathy for the Cubans' cause and African Americans' loyalty to the Republican Party extending back to the time of Lincoln, it was less enthusiastic about American expansion. Some African Americans saw opportunities in empire denied to them in the nation, but others associated their struggles with those of anticolonial nationalists in the Philippines and elsewhere. This article was published in The Broad Ax, *a Salt Lake City newspaper edited by former slave Julius F. Taylor. In contrast to most newspapers aimed at African American readers,* The Broad Ax *favored the Democrats, claiming that the Republicans had strayed from their earlier principles.*

"As Others See Us," *The Broad Ax* (Salt Lake City, Utah), May 16, 1899.

Several editors . . . and some of our readers have taken us to task because we have not been an enthusiastic supporter of President McKinley and the war policy which he has pursued in the Philippine Islands. If the editors and those of our readers would stop and reflect they could not consistently condemn us for refusing to lend aid and comfort to the American forces who are now engaged in murdering the inoffensive and liberty loving Filipinos.

The chief reasons why we are opposed to the war which is being waged upon the inhabitants of those islands are that whenever the soldiers send letters home to their relatives and parents they all breathe an utter contempt "for the niggers which they are engaged in slaying." Many of these letters have found their way into the columns of the press and without exception from the highest to the lowest the writers set forth in glowing colors "the number of niggers they have succeeded in putting to the sword." . . .

In view of these facts, no negro possessing any race pride can enter heartily into the prosecution of the war against the Filipinos, and all enlightened negroes must necessarily arrive at the conclusion that the war is being waged solely for greed and gold and not in the interest of suffering humanity. For if it were waged in the interest of the latter, the American soldiers would not turn up their noses and look down with scorn and contempt upon the Filipinos.

30

CARL SCHURZ

Colonies Are Not Necessary for the Expansion of Trade

1899

Carl Schurz immigrated to the United States from the autocratic state of Prussia following his participation in the failed Revolution of 1848. A staunch opponent of slavery, he rose in the ranks of the Republican Party, becoming the U.S. envoy to Spain, a U.S. senator from Missouri,

Carl Schurz, "American Imperialism," in *Republic or Empire? The Philippine Question,* ed. William Jennings Bryan et al. (Chicago: The Independence Company, 1899), 352–63.

and secretary of the interior. Schurz did not object to all forms of U.S. expansion—indeed, he favored the annexation of Canada—but as a senator he voted against treaties to acquire the Dominican Republic and Hawai'i, arguing that tropical peoples could not be assimilated into the United States as equals. Holding subject populations, he argued, would undermine American democracy. In the following remarks, he responds to claims that colonial policies would have economic payoffs. (See Document 26.)

The cry suddenly raised that this great country has become too small for us is too ridiculous to demand an answer, in view of the fact that our present population may be tripled and still have ample elbow-room, with resources to support many more. But we are told that our industries are gasping for breath; that we are suffering from over-production; that our products must have new outlets, and that we need colonies and dependencies the world over to give us more markets. More markets? Certainly. But do we, civilized beings, indulge in the absurd and barbarous notion that we must own the countries with which we wish to trade? . . .

There is a distinguished Englishman, the Right Hon. Charles T. Ritchie, President of the Board of Trade, telling a British Chamber of Commerce that "we (Great Britain) are being rapidly overhauled in exports by other nations, especially the United States and Germany," their exports fast advancing, while British exports are declining. What? Great Britain, the greatest colonial power in the world, losing in competition with two nations, one of which had, so far, no colonies or dependencies at all, and the other none of any commercial importance? What does this mean? It means that, as proved by the United States and Germany, colonies are not necessary for the expansion of trade, and that, as proved by Great Britain, colonies do not protect a nation against a loss of trade. Our trade expands, without colonies or big navies, because we produce certain goods better and in proportion cheaper than other people do. British trade declines, in spite of immense dependencies and the strongest navy, because it does not successfully compete with us in that respect. Trade follows, not the flag, but the best goods for the price. Expansion of export trade and new markets! We do not need foreign conquests to get them, for we have them, and are getting them more and more in rapidly increasing growth.

"But the Pacific Ocean," we are mysteriously told, "will be the great commercial battlefield of the future, and we must quickly use the present opportunity to secure our position on it. The visible presence of great power is necessary for us to get our share of the trade of China. Therefore we must have the Philippines." Well, the China trade is worth having, although for a time out of sight the Atlantic Ocean will be an infinitely more important battlefield of commerce than the Pacific, and one European customer is worth more than twenty or thirty Asiatics. But does the trade of China really require that we should have the Philippines and make a great display of power to get our share? Read the consular reports, and you will find that in many places in China our trade is rapidly gaining, while in some British trade is declining, and this while Great Britain had on hand the greatest display of power imaginable and we had none. And in order to increase our trade there, our consuls advise us to improve our commercial methods, saying nothing of the necessity of establishing a base of naval operations, and of our appearing there with war ships and heavy guns. Trade is developed, not by the best guns, but by the best merchants. But why do other nations prepare to fight for the Chinese trade? Other nations have done many foolish things which we have been, and I hope will remain, wise enough not to imitate. If it should come to fighting for Chinese customers, the powers engaged in that fight are not unlikely to find out that they pay too high a price for what can be gained, and that at last the peaceful and active neutral will have the best bargain. At any rate, to launch into all the embroilments of an imperialistic policy by annexing the Philippines in order to snatch something more of the Chinese trade would be for us the foolishest game of all. . . .

"But we must have coaling stations for our navy!" Well, can we not get as many coaling stations as we need without owning populous countries behind them that would entangle us in dangerous political responsibilities and complications?

31

JOSEPH HENRY CROOKER

Is This the Gospel of Jesus?

1900

Joseph Henry Crooker was a Unitarian minister and temperance activist who objected to imperialists' claims that the United States was doing God's work in the Philippines. The Bible was not his only source of inspiration, however. Crooker's warning about "cheap Asiatic workmen" drew on the rhetoric of union leaders such as Samuel Gompers, who warned that Asian workers would travel from the Philippines to the United States, thereby lowering wages for white working men.

A political doctrine is now preached in our midst that is the most alarming evidence of moral decay that ever appeared in American history. Its baleful significance consists, not simply in its moral hatefulness, but in the fact that its advocates are so numerous and so prominent.

It is this: A powerful nation, representative of civilization, has the right, for the general good of humanity, to buy, conquer, subjugate, control, and govern feeble and backward races and peoples, without reference to their wishes or opinions.

This is preached from pulpits as the gospel of Christ. It is proclaimed in executive documents as American statesmanship. It is defended in legislative halls as the beginning of a more glorious chapter in human history. It is boastfully declaimed from the platform as the first great act in the regeneration of mankind. It is published in innumerable editorials, red with cries for blood and hot with lust for gold, as the call of God to the American people.

But how came these men to know so clearly the mind of the Almighty? Was the cant of piety ever more infamously used? Was selfishness ever more wantonly arrayed in the vestments of sanctity? Is this the modern chivalry of the strong to the weak? Then let us surrender all our fair ideals and admit that might alone makes right. Is this the duty of great

Joseph Henry Crooker, *The Menace to America* (Chicago: American Anti-imperialist League, 1900), 3–4, 10.

nations to small peoples? Then morality is a fiction. Is this the gospel of Jesus? Then let us repudiate the Golden Rule. Is this the crowning lesson of America to the world? Then let us renounce our democracy. . . .

It is pitiful that our people, and especially the common people, should be so carried away by wild and baseless dreams of the commercial advantage of these Islands. It is bad enough to sacrifice patriotism upon the altar of Mammon;[1] but it is clear that in this case the sacrifice will be made without securing any benefit, even from Mammon.

The annual expense our Nation will incur by the military and naval establishment in the Philippines will be at least $100,000,000. This the taxpayer of America must pay. On the other hand, the trade profits from these Islands—from the very nature of the case—will go directly into the pockets of millionaire monopolists, the few speculators who will get possession of the business interests there, in the line of hemp, sugar, tobacco and lumber.

The proposition is a plain one. These Islands will cost us, the common people, a hundred million dollars a year. The profits from them, possibly an equal sum, will go directly to a few very rich men. This is a very sleek speculative scheme for transferring vast sums of money from the people at large to the bank accounts of a few monopolists. Can any one see anything very helpful to the common taxpayer in such a policy? This is a serious problem for consideration, in addition to the competition of American labor with cheap Asiatic workmen—in itself sufficiently serious.

[1] A New Testament reference to the false god of wealth.

32

VARINA DAVIS

What Are We Going to Do with These Additional Millions of Negroes?

1900

Varina Davis, once the first lady of the Confederacy, supported herself after the Civil War by writing. Many of her articles romanticized the southern "lost cause." In this document, she brings her understanding of southern race relations to bear on U.S. policies in the Philippines. As many as a third of the participants in some anti-imperialist rallies were women, many motivated by more liberal commitments to equal rights than Davis expressed. The visibility of women in the anti-imperialist cause led imperialists to discredit their opponents as effeminate "aunties" who were unsuited to participate in what they saw as the inherently masculine world of politics.

My most serious objection to making the Philippines American territory is because three-fourths of the population is made up of negroes. I understand that the people form a sort of human mosaic, representing the mixture of a number of tribes, nationalities, and races. Even the different native races are an admixture of many grades of Indians and blacks. Added to these are hundreds of thousands of half-castes between the various native types and the Spaniards; and so numerous are these blends that even natives themselves can hardly identify a particular type. You may call them Christianized Malays, if you will, but pure blood of any sort is said to be rare. . . .

The question is, What are we going to do with these additional millions of negroes? Civilize them? You might bring all the processes of civilization to bear upon the negro, and you may educate him; but, except in isolated cases, you cannot make him thrifty. After the negro has acquired knowledge, he usually does not know how best to apply it; and

Mrs. Jefferson Davis [Varina Davis], "Why We Do Not Want the Philippines," *Arena* 23 (January 1900): 2, 4.

advocates of the higher education of the race have been in many cases grievously disappointed in the outcome of their best efforts, though certainly among the race there are striking exceptions that only prove the rule. The sympathies of the Southern people have always been with their former slaves; but the influence of pernicious books and low white associates, a very partial education, and no self-control have changed a kind and simple-hearted people in some cases into a semi-savage and predatory class. . . .

When the revolt in the Philippines shall have been suppressed, we will have on our hands a very large population of negroes, or half-breeds, who are more ignorant and more degraded than those in our Southern States. Of course, this remark does not apply to the educated and refined class of the Filipinos, of whom there are quite a number—even those of mixed blood. What are we to do with this mighty negro population, who do not speak our language and come to us in enforced citizenship and full of smoldering discontent? . . .

I see only one solution to the problem. Give the Filipinos the right to govern themselves under certain restrictions, commercial and otherwise, and refuse to burden the United States with fresh millions of foreign negroes whose standards are different and whose language is alien—at least until we have solved the race problem here at home.

7

Colonial Governance

33

RICHARD P. LEARY

Licentious and Lawless Conduct in Guam

1900

The USS Charleston *arrived at the Spanish possession of Guam in June 1898 and seized it for use as a coaling station. The* Charleston *soon steamed off to fight in the Philippines, but the following year, Richard P. Leary took up his post as Guam's first U.S. Navy governor. Aside from the Japanese occupation during World War II, the U.S. Navy continued to govern Guam and its indigenous Chamorro people until 1950, when the island was reorganized as an unincorporated U.S. territory, a status it maintains today.*

General Order No. 11

1. It is to be regretted that the licentious and lawless conduct of some of the men belonging to this station has made it necessary to issue this order, which is intended to be a reminder that in assuming control of this island the Government is pledged to fulfill its guarantee of absolute protection of all the rights and privileges of the residents of Guam in their homes and in their lawful pursuits of life.

2. Attention is hereby called to the fact that the natives of Guam are not "damned dagoes" nor "niggers," but they are law-abiding, respectful human beings, who have been taken under the protection of the United

Brig. General Joseph Wheeler, *Report on the Island of Guam*, War Department, Adjutant-General's Office, report 28 (Washington, D.C.: Government Printing Office, 1900).

States Government and who are as much entitled to courtesy, respect, and protection of life and liberty in their homes and in their occupations as are the best citizens of New York, Washington, or any other home city.

3. The several disgraceful cases of assault, committed by persons attached to this station, interfering with the functions of local officials, ruthlessly destroying private property, viciously violating the sanctity of native homes, etc., were worthy only of the dastardly cowards and blackguards who were implicated in those acts, and it is deeply regretted that the Government has thus far been unable to sufficiently establish the identity of the culprits and their abettors in order that they might be brought to justice.

4. For the preservation of the well-earned reputation of the American Navy as champions in succoring the needy, aiding the distressed, and protecting the honor and virtue of women, it is earnestly hoped that the honorable, self-respecting portion of this command will unite their efforts in using all lawful means within their power to discourage and suppress every known tendency on the part of others to commit lawless acts that would cast dishonor and shame on the service in which we have shared the honors and trials of wars and to which we have dedicated our official lives.

34

HENRY BILLINGS BROWN

A Territory Appurtenant and Belonging to the United States

1901

The Downes v. Bidwell *case was one of about twenty cases heard by the U.S. Supreme Court between 1900 and 1922 that came to be known as the Insular Cases because they addressed the legal status of the island territories acquired in the Caribbean and the Pacific. On the narrowest level,* Downes *pertained to whether a New York fruit importer should pay duty on oranges from San Juan. In a broader sense,* Downes *decided*

[Justice Henry Billings Brown], *Downes v. Bidwell*, 182 U.S. 244 (1901), Supreme Court of the United States. Argued January 8–11, 1901. Decided May 27, 1901.

whether Puerto Rico fell within the United States. By a one-vote margin,
the Court acknowledged that Puerto Rico had ceased to be a foreign coun-
try. Yet the Court also found that "unincorporated" territories need not
receive the same constitutional protections as "incorporated" territories.
The author of the Downes *decision, Justice Henry Billings Brown, is*
better known for his "separate but equal" decision in Plessy v. Ferguson
(1896), yet it is his Downes *decision that still stands.*

Congress did not hesitate, in the original organization of the territories of
Louisiana, Florida, the Northwest Territory, and its subdivisions of Ohio,
Indiana, Michigan, Illinois and Wisconsin, and still more recently in the
case of Alaska, to establish a form of government bearing a much greater
analogy to a British crown colony than a republican State of America, and
to vest the legislative power either in a governor and council, or a governor and judges, to be appointed by the President. It was not until they
had attained a certain population that power was given them to organize
a legislature by vote of the people. In all these cases, as well as in Territories subsequently organized west of the Mississippi, Congress thought it
necessary either to extend the Constitution and laws in the United States
over them, or to declare that the inhabitants should be entitled to enjoy
the right of trial by jury, of bail, and of the privilege of the writ of *habeas
corpus,* as well as other privileges of the bill of rights.

We are also of opinion that the power to acquire territory by treaty
implies not only the power to govern such territory, but to prescribe
upon what terms the United States will receive its inhabitants, and what
their *status* shall be in what Chief Justice [John] Marshall termed the
"American Empire." There seems to be no middle ground between this
position and the doctrine that if their inhabitants do not become, immediately upon annexation, citizens of the United States, their children
thereafter born, whether savages or civilized, are such, and entitled to
all the rights, privileges and immunities of citizens. If such be their *status,* the consequences will be extremely serious. Indeed, it is doubtful if
Congress would ever assent to the annexation of territory upon the condition that its inhabitants, however foreign they may be to our habits,
traditions and modes of life, shall become at once citizens of the United
States. In all its treaties hitherto the treaty-making power has made special provision for this subject; in the cases of Louisiana and Florida, by
stipulating that "the inhabitants shall be incorporated in the Union of
the United States and admitted as soon as possible . . . to the enjoyment

of all the rights, advantages and immunities of citizens of the United States," in the case of Mexico, that they should "be incorporated into the Union, and be admitted at the proper time, (to be judged of by the Congress of the United States,) to the enjoyment of all the rights of citizens of the United States," in the case of Alaska, that the inhabitants who remained three years, "with the exception of uncivilized native tribes, shall be admitted to the enjoyment of all the rights," etc.; and in the case of Porto Rico and the Philippines, "that the civil rights and political *status* of the native inhabitants . . . shall be determined by Congress." In all these cases there is an implied denial of the right of the inhabitants to American citizenship until Congress by further action shall signify its assent thereto. . . .

Patriotic and intelligent men may differ widely as to the desireableness of this or that acquisition, but this is solely a political question. We can only consider this aspect of the case so far as to say that no construction of the Constitution should be adopted which would prevent Congress from considering each case upon its merits, unless the language of the instrument imperatively demand it. A false step at this time might be fatal to the development of what Chief Justice Marshall called the American Empire. Choice in some cases, the natural gravitation of small bodies towards large ones in others, the result of a successful war in still others, may bring about conditions which would render the annexation of distant possessions desirable. If those possessions are inhabited by alien races, differing from us in religion, customs, laws, methods of taxation and modes of thought, the administration of government and justice, according to Anglo-Saxon principles, may for a time be impossible; and the question at once arises whether large concessions ought not to be made for a time, that, ultimately, our own theories may be carried out, and the blessings of a free government under the Constitution extended to them. We decline to hold that there is anything in the Constitution to forbid such action.

We are therefore of opinion that the Island of Porto Rico is a territory appurtenant and belonging to the United States, but not a part of the United States within the revenue clauses of the Constitution; that the Foraker[1] act is constitutional, so far as it imposes duties upon imports from such island, and that the plaintiff cannot recover back the duties exacted in this case.

---

[1] The 1900 act establishing a civilian government in Puerto Rico and extending U.S. federal laws to the island.

35

ROBERTO H. TODD ET AL.

Porto Rico Enslaved

1905

The first U.S. military governor of Puerto Rico, General John R. Brooke, earned the enmity of many Puerto Ricans by suppressing their parliament and intervening in their judicial system. Although Puerto Ricans objected to the reduction of the political rights they had exercised under Spanish rule, they disagreed on how to move forward. Wealthy sugar and coffee producers eager for greater access to U.S. markets saw annexation as personally advantageous, as did some working people who had the opposite expectation: that U.S. rule would liberate them from elite oppression. Yet even Puerto Ricans who called for eventual statehood demanded full self-government and universal male suffrage in the meantime. This message to the U.S. Congress was signed by ninety-seven municipal council delegates from fifty-two Puerto Rican towns.

Seven years ago to-day, the 25th of July, the American Army invaded this country by the port of Guanica. We knew the history and tradition of your country; we knew that the flag of your nation forever floated over worthy homes and dignified communities. The landing of your soldiers meant to us the further enlargement of the horizon of our public life.

Shortly before that time the nation that discovered this country, having theretofore granted to the inhabitants of Porto Rico the same political rights as to the inhabitants of the Spanish peninsula, had acknowledged the principle of self-government in our local administration, and it was natural, therefore, that we should have felt confident that the invading nation would not lessen the scope of that principle, especially in the view of your own declaration that the war of 1898 was waged for the purpose of liberating countries which were being ruled over by tyranny. Coupled to the logic of this conclusion was our faith in you and in your democratic principles, and your armies were hailed with a cry of joy from south to

Memorial of July 25, 1905, submitted by the delegates from Puerto Rican municipal councils, *Hearings before the Committee on Pacific Islands and Porto Rico, United States Senate*, February 6, 1906, consideration of bill S. 2620, 10–12.

north Porto Rico. No hostile resistance was made, but instead the way was open for a complete moral conquest.

A government by the sword established by the President of the United States lasted twenty-eight months. We waited for you, American legislators, to speak, and at last you did speak on the 12th day of April, 1900, creating, by the Foraker Act, a house of delegates elected by the people and an executive council with legislative and executive powers, appointed by the President of the United States under the condition that the Porto Ricans were to have in the last-named body a minimum representation of five members, and this minimum has never been increased, for the American members have always been six and the several departments in which the administration is divided have always been under their charge.

In opposition to the most simple principles of political law obtaining, without a single exception, in countries under a parliamentary system of government, such as France or Great Britain, or under a representative system, such as that of your own country, the legislative and executive powers are merged in the executive council, the majority of which, composed of the six heads of departments, heretofore Americans, are the arbiters in the passage of our laws. . . . Thus the six Americans appointed by the President have had greater power than the thirty-five representatives of the island in the house of delegates and the five Porto Rican members of the council—in other words, they have had more power than the whole people of Porto Rico. . . .

For that reason we are here to-day, speaking on behalf of our municipalities; for that reason, in view of the anti-American sentiment which is beginning to develop in Porto Rico, we appeal to you for assistance in checking and exterminating such sentiment, as you are the only ones competent to accomplish such a grand work. Porto Rico desires the sovereignty of the United States; but it does not desire the tutelage which the officers of the insular administration exercise over it.

Neither the Congress nor the people of the United States will turn a deaf ear to the voice of a poor, weak people, but on the contrary, will take into consideration that the example set in Porto Rico is being constantly watched from Cuba, Mexico, and the Central and South American republics, and if such an example be not satisfactory to our brothers of Latin origin it will become more and more difficult to establish the political and commercial hegemony to which the United States are entitled by their position, population, and civilization. An experiment is being made in our island. Porto Rico happy and contented means a great current of sympathy flowing from south to north in the Western Hemisphere, which we inhabit. A discontented, despairing Porto Rico means a current of opposite sentiments.

Porto Rico enslaved means Central and South America alarmed and suspicious; it means the expansion policy, smooth and spontaneous, retarding or curtailing its beneficial attractions; it means the Monroe doctrine, or, in other words, the solidarity of the peoples of the three Americas—North, Central, and South—strained by jealousy instead of approaching amidst praises and blessings. . . .

Pray grant unto this country all legislative authority and at the same time all responsibility. We can not accept that public officers be sent to Porto Rico who, as a general rule, are unacquainted with the language, the customs, and the needs of this country, and within twenty-four hours after their arrival take their seats in the executive council and decide by their votes complicated and transcendental questions. We desire that the opportunity, heretofore denied to us, be given that we may show that we are now capable of self-government. Our commonwealth has an old civilization of its own; we have shown our estimation and respect for the laws; we worked out the problem of the abolition of slavery within the most perfect normal bounds; we have met without disorder most terrible financial crises. We know ourselves, we fully know our needs, and we are fully convinced that we can successfully manage our own local affairs.

36

H. C. THEOBALD

Clean Bodies and Clean Clothes

1907

The U.S. Army began organizing schools, with soldiers as teachers, during the Philippine-American War. The goal was to convince the Filipinos—only about 45 percent of whom were literate in any language—of U.S. benevolence. Later, the United States sent over a thousand trained teachers to the Philippines, many of them attracted by higher salaries than they could earn at home. The various superintendents put different emphases on education,

H. C. Theobald, *The Filipino Teacher's Manual* (New York: World Book, 1907), 62, 64–65, 200–201.

which shifted from basic literacy for the masses to manual training (weaving, gardening, woodworking, sewing, pottery, and the like) and then to better secondary instruction, albeit for fewer students. Colonial educators also prioritized English-language instruction. H. C. Theobald served as principal of the Batangas Provincial High School. (On education, see also Documents 8, 10, and 43.)

The school water-closets, one for girls and one for boys, at proper distances from each other and from the schoolhouse, should be larger than those for single families, but constructed upon the same plan: a shallow vault; a light building with poles attached so that it may be lifted and carried by four men; and for each closet a box of earth, ashes, or lime, with a little shovel for depositing the earth in the vault. The teacher should inspect the closets daily, and have them moved to a new place when it is necessary. He should try also to have the more permanent modern closet supplied for the school. He should be progressive, and content with nothing but the best. . . .

The teacher should observe very closely the health of the pupils of his school. One of the first things that he should demand in his school is personal cleanliness. Some children, when they begin to attend school, need to be taught to keep themselves clean. Those who are unwashed, and whose clothes are dirty, should not be allowed to remain in such a condition. Every child must be taught to change his shirt at least once a week. If the country boy has but one abacá[1] shirt, he must sometimes stay at home long enough to have it washed and ironed. Children with dirty hands and dirty faces should be sent to the river or to the well. The teacher may praise cleanliness and neatness, but it is unwise to call attention to a pupil whose appearance is not neat and clean. A better plan is to take the boy aside and speak to him quietly; for he may not be to blame. Fine clothes are not suitable for work or business, and poor children cannot afford fine clothes for any occasion; but clean bodies and clean clothes may be had by all. . . .

Our aims in the schools of the Philippines must be *to unite book-learning with industrial training. Every boy and every girl should know some useful trade.* This does not mean that he or she will be compelled to work at that trade through life, but that whatever happens to them, the boy and the girl will have some means of making a living. More than

---

[1] A textile made from Manila hemp.

this, they will learn to honor all kinds of industry. In the past, a very wrong idea grew up in the minds of the people. This was the idea that learning gained in schools should separate the boys and girls from the farmers and the manufacturers, and from those who work with their hands. Those who were educated were expected to become lawyers, doctors, office-holders, or teachers. So the people did not honor any occupation that made the hands rough and dirty.

By teaching trades and industries in the schools, we shall give dignity to every occupation that produces wealth for the nation, whether it be carpentry, iron-working, mat-weaving, wood-carving, hat-making, pottery work, or shoemaking. This is not all the good that will come from industrial teaching; we must remember that a hard-working people is generally a strong, healthy race. . . . Better homes and better food will also result from the ability to earn good wages. These better conditions of life will cause crime and vice to grow less. Finally, it may be stated that greater production will so increase the national resources that taxes will no longer be burdensome.

With many lines of industrial training carried on seriously and persistently in the schools, a great army of young workers will soon be formed. Within ten or fifteen years, there will be no need of talking about laws to permit workers from foreign countries to enter the Philippines. There will be thousands of young Filipinos prepared by their training to take up the various trades. The development of the islands by the Filipinos themselves will be seen in every province. "The Philippines for the Filipinos," as a policy of the government, must be carried out by the Filipinos—but they cannot carry out this policy *except by preparing themselves to take up all the kinds of hard work* that are necessary in building up a modern nation.

37

EDITH MOSES

The Filipinos Are like Children
1908

Edith Moses came to the Philippines with her husband, a member of
the Second Philippine Commission, which was charged with setting up
a civilian colonial government. The colonial powers had long held up
white women as partners in the colonizing project, responsible for keeping
white men from the corruption of native concubines and with modeling
middle-class morality and housekeeping. The wives of colonial officials
also advanced U.S. interests by participating in the social events that
smoothed relations with the Filipino elite.

Manila, June 11, 1900

Last week we began cleaning and painting, and ever since our house has
been full of Filipinos who have somehow become part of our household
in this easy-going place. I have gained quite an insight into native character through this experience. The Filipinos are like children and love
to do everything but the thing they are set to do. They run to assist the
house boys in their work; they advise me about arranging my furniture;
and insist upon unpacking china when they are hired to paint the walls.
They are always playing tricks on each other, and are unfailingly good-
natured, but the painting progresses very slowly; often they disappear
altogether, but come back again smiling next day, explaining it was a
fiesta. From an ethnological standpoint this is all interesting, but I can
imagine that here is displayed one of the race characteristics, which,
after the novelty is gone, "weareth the Christian down." . . .

. . . Manila is a tranquil city. Political affairs are much more encouraging than they seemed to be when we left America. All organized resistance is over. There are a great many bandits and robbers, but every day
they are being captured and their ammunition discovered. The dreaded
rainy season is worse for the Filipinos than for our men, for now we hold

---

Edith Moses, *Unofficial Letters of an Official's Wife* (New York: D. Appleton, 1908), 16–17,
33–34, 221–26.

all the towns and they are "chasing themselves around the country," as a young officer put it. They do not seem to be such a fierce race as they are reported. They strike me as lazy, polite, and good-natured. They may be treacherous, and everyone says they are, but on the surface the lower classes are certainly very agreeable.

We have a neighbor opposite who lives in a nipa hut.[1] He has a wife and two children, and is a fisherman. Once or twice we have thrown candy out of the window to the children. Last Sunday morning the little girl came up the stairway leading her small brother by the hand. He wore a gauze shirt that came about two inches below his armpits. The little girl wore a pink calico chemise and carried in her hand a plate of fresh crabs. This was a gift in return for the candy. I offered to pay for them but she ran away, shaking her head. . . .

Manila, March 23, 1902

I suppose the correspondents have telegraphed to America the news of the outbreak of cholera, and that you are imagining all sorts of horrors. The fact is that after the first uncertainty—during the days when the authorities suspected its existence, but were hoping the disease would be sporadic—we were all more or less nervous, but now that we know that Manila is really in for a siege of cholera, everyone has calmed down, and is hard at work making the town as sanitary as possible. The excitement attending so serious a situation as the outbreak of cholera, in a city in which only a few years ago thirty thousand persons perished within three months, keeps one from taking time to be frightened. . . . We hosed off the "China" boys and Filipinos with disinfectants, and I made their eyes stick out with fright by describing a cholera germ. . . . Of course, we eat only tinned vegetables and well-done meats, but in addition we toast all the bread, heat all the plates, and scald all the glasses before every meal. We open a fresh tin of cream each meal, and have concluded to buy tinned butter. The water is distilled, and the bottles in which we keep it sterilized. This means continuous oversight, and at night I am so tired that I have no time to let my imagination run riot.

The Commission is holding extra sessions, and everyone is working to prevent the spread of the disease, and get the city in as sanitary a condition as possible. It has been divided into districts, in each of which there is a chief surgeon, under whom are doctors, inspectors, police, and helpers. There is a house-to-house inspection, and the nipa shacks

---

[1] A stilt house, made in part from nipa palm leaves.

in which deaths occur are to be burned, because the nipa hut cannot be properly disinfected. The government will pay the owners for the property destroyed. A detention camp has been built outside the city, where it is proposed to detain the inmates of the houses where a death from cholera has occurred. This quarantine camp is regarded with suspicion by the natives, who imagine all kinds of horrors await them there. It is difficult to manage the lowest classes, who are the ones at present in the greatest danger. They instinctively hide their sick, and do everything to avoid a quarantine. Even intelligent Filipinos are disposed to conceal the fact that a member of their family has cholera. One reason is the prohibition of funerals, and the fear of cremation, which they seem to think will send them straight to perdition.

Manila, April 4, 1902

. . . . We are still fighting the cholera, but, as the natives persist in hiding the sick, the number of cases is increasing. The Board of Health is burning whole districts where the shacks are in a filthy condition. It is hard for the natives; they are bewildered, and cannot understand the reason for it. Some one said the other night that the natives were more afraid of the sanitary inspector than of the cholera. Sometimes, when I think of our rough ways of doing things, I feel an intense pity for these poor people, who are being what we call "civilized" by main force. Of course, in the cholera time it is for their immediate good, and the government pays for their houses and their goods, yet they cannot understand it, and it seems an act of tyranny worse than that of the Spaniards.

38

JAMES WELDON JOHNSON

The Truth about the Conquest of Haiti

1920

James Weldon Johnson served as a U.S. consul in Venezuela and Nicaragua, helping in the latter post to suppress revolutionary activity opposed by U.S. corporate interests. He later dedicated himself to writing and in 1920 became the executive secretary of the National Association for the Advancement of Colored People. One of the issues he addressed was the U.S. occupation of Haiti, which lasted from 1915 to 1934. This document is excerpted from an article titled "Self-Determining Haiti"—an ironic reference to President Woodrow Wilson's calls for national self-determination in Europe.

The law by which Haiti is ruled today is martial law dispensed by Americans. There is a form of Haitian civil government, but it is entirely dominated by the military Occupation. President Dartiguenave,[1] bitterly rebellious at heart as is every good Haitian, confessed to me the powerlessness of himself and his cabinet. He told me that the American authorities give no heed to recommendations made by him or his officers; that they would not even discuss matters about which the Haitian officials have superior knowledge. The provisions of both the old and the new constitutions are ignored in that there is no Haitian legislative body, and there has been none since the dissolution of the assembly in April, 1916. In its stead there is a Council of State composed of twenty-one members appointed by the president, which functions effectively only when carrying out the will of the Occupation. Indeed the Occupation often overrides the civil courts. A prisoner brought before the proper court, exonerated, and discharged, is, nevertheless, frequently held by the military. All government funds are collected by the Occupation and are dispensed at its

---

[1]Philippe Sudré Dartiguenave, president of Haiti from 1915 to 1922.

James Weldon Johnson, "Self-Determining Haiti, I. The American Occupation," *The Nation* 111 (August 28, 1920): 237–38; "Self-Determining Haiti, II. What the United States Has Accomplished," *The Nation* 111 (September 4, 1920): 265–67.

will and pleasure. The greater part of these funds is expended for the maintenance of the military forces. There is the strictest censorship of the press. No Haitian newspaper is allowed to publish anything in criticism of the Occupation or the Haitian government. Each newspaper in Haiti received an order to that effect from the Occupation, *and the same order carried the injunction not to print the order*. Nothing that might reflect upon the Occupation administration in Haiti is allowed to reach the newspapers of the United States. . . .

. . . The military Occupation has made and continues to make military Occupation necessary. The justification given is that it is necessary for the pacification of the country. Pacification would never have been necessary had not American policies been filled with so many stupid and brutal blunders; and it will never be effective so long as "pacification" means merely the hunting of ragged Haitians in the hills with machine guns.

Then there is the force which the several hundred American civilian place-holders constitute. They have found in Haiti the veritable promised land of "jobs for deserving democrats" and naturally do not wish to see the present status discontinued. Most of these deserving democrats are Southerners. The head of the customs service of Haiti was a clerk of one of the parishes of Louisiana. Second in charge of the customs service of Haiti is a man who was Deputy Collector of Customs at Pascagoula, Mississippi (population, 3,379, 1910 Census). The Superintendent of Public Instruction was a school teacher in Louisiana—a State which has not good schools even for white children. . . .

Many of the Occupation officers are in the same category with the civilian place-holders. These men have taken their wives and families to Haiti. Those at Port-au-Prince live in beautiful villas. Families that could not keep a hired girl in the United States have a half-dozen servants. They ride in automobiles—not their own. Every American head of a department in Haiti has an automobile furnished at the expense of the Haitian Government, whereas members of the Haitian cabinet, who are theoretically above them, have no such convenience or luxury. While I was there, the President himself was obliged to borrow an automobile from the Occupation for a trip through the interior. The Louisiana school-teacher Superintendent of Instruction has an automobile furnished at government expense, whereas the Haitian Minister of Public Instruction, his supposed superior officer, has none. These automobiles seem to be chiefly employed in giving the women and children an airing each afternoon. It must be amusing, when it is not maddening to the Haitians, to see with what disdainful air these people look upon them as they ride by. . . .

When the truth about the conquest of Haiti—the slaughter of three thousand and practically unarmed Haitians, with the incidentally needless death of a score of American boys—begins to filter through the rigid Administration censorship to the American people, the apologists will become active. Their justification of what has been done will be grouped under two heads: one, the necessity, and two, the results. Under the first, much stress will be laid upon the "anarchy" which existed in Haiti, upon the backwardness of the Haitians and their absolute unfitness to govern themselves. . . . Now as to results: The apologists will attempt to show that material improvements in Haiti justify American intervention. Let us see what they are.

Diligent inquiry reveals just three: The building of the road from Port-au-Prince to Cape Haitien; the enforcement of certain sanitary regulations in the larger cities; and the improvement of the public hospital at Port-au-Prince. The enforcement of certain sanitary regulations is not so important as it may sound, for even under exclusive native rule, Haiti has been a remarkably healthy country and had never suffered from such epidemics as used to sweep Cuba and the Panama Canal region. The regulations, moreover, were of a purely minor character—the sort that might be issued by a board of health in any American city or town—and were in no wise fundamental, because there was no need. The same applies to the improvement of the hospital, long before the American Occupation, an effectively conducted institution but which, it is only fair to say, benefited considerably by the regulations and more up-to-date methods of American army surgeons—the best in the world. Neither of these accomplishments, however, creditable as they are, can well be put forward as a justification for military domination. The building of the great highway from Port-au-Prince to Cape Haitien is a monumental piece of work, but it is doubtful whether the object in building it was to supply the Haitians with a great highway or to construct a military road which would facilitate the transportation of troops and supplies from one end of the island to the other. And this represents the sum total of the constructive accomplishment after five years of American Occupation.

Now, the highway, while doubtless the most important achievement of the three, involved the most brutal of all the blunders of the Occupation. The work was in charge of an officer of Marines who stands out even in that organization for his "treat 'em rough" methods. He discovered the obsolete Haitian *corvée*, or road law, in Haiti provided that each citizen should work a certain number of days on the public roads to keep them in condition, or pay a certain sum of money. In the days when this law was in force the Haitian government never required the men to work the roads except in their respective communities, and the number of days was usually limited to three a year. But the Occupation seized men wherever it could find them, and no able-bodied Haitian was safe from such raids, which most closely resembled the African slave raids of past centuries. And slavery it was—though temporary. By day or by night, from the bosom of their families, from their little farms or while trudging peacefully on the country roads, Haitians were seized and forcibly taken to toil for months in far sections of the country. Those who protested or resisted were beaten into submission. At night, after long hours of unremitting labor under armed taskmasters, who swiftly discouraged any slackening of effort with boot or rifle butt, the victims were herded into compounds. Those attempting to escape were shot. Their terror-stricken families meanwhile were often in total ignorance of the fate of their husbands, fathers, brothers. . . .

The completed highway, moreover, continued to be a barb in the Haitian wound. Automobiles on this road, running without any speed limit, are a constant inconvenience or danger to the natives carrying their market produce to town on their heads or loaded on the backs of animals. I have seen these people scramble in terror often up the side or down the declivity of the mountain for places of safety for themselves and their animals as the machines snorted by. I have seen a market woman's horse take flight and scatter the produce loaded on his back all over the road for several hundred yards. I have heard an American commercial traveler laughingly tell how on the trip from Cape Haitien to Port-au-Prince the automobile he was in killed a donkey and two pigs. It had not occurred to him that the donkey might be the chief capital of the small Haitian farmer and that the loss of it might entirely bankrupt him. . . .

Perhaps the most serious aspect of American brutality in Haiti is not to be found in individual cases of cruelty, numerous and inexcusable though they are, but rather in the American attitude, well illustrated by the diagnosis of an American officer discussing the situation and its difficulty: "The trouble with this whole business is that some of these people with a little money and education think they are as good as we are," and this is the keynote of the attitude of every American to every Haitian. Americans have carried American hatred to Haiti. They have planted the feeling of caste and color prejudice where it never before existed.

8

Race Making in Colonial Contexts

39

U.S. STATISTICS BUREAU

Wages in Hawaii

1899

Despite claims that land privatization would benefit ordinary Hawai'ians, less than 1 percent of the islands' land passed to Hawai'ian commoners following the 1848 Māhele land division. Finding the Hawai'ian labor supply insufficient for their demands, the outside investors who acquired much of Hawai'i's land sought immigrant labor for their plantations. In 1870, Native Hawai'ians constituted 88 percent of the islands' people; by 1900, only 24 percent. The remaining population consisted mostly of Japanese (40 percent), Chinese (17 percent), Portuguese (10 percent), and U.S. (5 percent) settlers. After 1898, planters also looked to the U.S. territories of Puerto Rico and the Philippines for workers. By 1916, more than twenty thousand Filipinos had gone to Hawai'i, generally under three-year labor contracts.

Wages

The following is an approximation of the wages paid to different classes of labor on the Hawaiian Islands:

Engineers on plantations, from \$125 to \$175 per month, house and firewood furnished.

U.S. Statistics Bureau, "The Hawaiian Islands," in *Foreign Commerce of Cuba, Puerto Rico, the Hawaiian, Philippine, and Samoan Islands* (Washington, D.C.: Government Printing Office, 1899), 1333.

Sugar boilers, $125 to $175 per month, house and firewood furnished.

Blacksmiths, plantation, $50 to $100 per month, house and firewood furnished.

Carpenters, plantation, $50 to $100 per month, house and firewood furnished.

Locomotive drivers, $40 to $75 per month, room and board furnished.

Head overseers, or head lunas,[1] $100 to $150.

Under overseers, or lunas, $30 to $50, with room and board.

Bookkeepers, plantation, $100 to $175, house and firewood furnished.

Teamsters, white, $30 to $40, with room and board.

Hawaiians, $25 to $30, with room; no board.

Field labor, Portuguese and Hawaiian, $16 to $18 per month; no board.

Field labor, Chinese and Japanese, $12.50 to $15 per month; no board.

In Honolulu bricklayers and masons receive from $5 to $6 per day; carpenters, $2.50 to $5; machinists, $3 to $5; painters, $2 to $5 per day, of nine hours.

Domestic Labor

The domestic labor in Honolulu and in all parts of the islands has for many years been performed by Chinese males, who undoubtedly make excellent house servants. During the last four or five years the Japanese have entered the field. The Japanese women are especially in demand as nurses for children.

The following are the prevailing rates of wages:

Cooks, Chinese and Japanese, $3 to $6 per week, with board and room.

Nurses and house servants, $8 to $12 per month, with board and room.

Gardeners or yard men, $8 to $12 per month, with board and room.

Sewing women, $1 per day and one meal.

Good substantial meals can be obtained at respectable Chinese restaurants and at the Sailors' Home for 25 cents, or board for $4.50 per week.

[1]Foremen.

40

SIXTO LOPEZ

The "Tribes" in the Philippines
1900

When war broke out between the United States and the nascent Philippine Republic, Sixto Lopez was in Washington, D.C., serving as secretary of the Philippine mission to the United States. After the United States refused to recognize the Philippine Republic, Lopez urged his compatriots to cease hostilities, arguing that armed resistance would not secure independence. Lopez wrote this essay in response to a cluster of imperialist claims: that the people of the Philippines were savages in need of civilizing, that the islands were too fragmented by tribe and ethnicity to successfully unite as a nation, and that the westernized Filipino political elite could not be entrusted with the task of safeguarding and uplifting non-Christian Filipinos.

There has been a considerable amount of speculation about the Negritos, who are erroneously regarded as the aboriginal inhabitants of the whole Archipelago. But Pedro A. Paterno, one of our most capable ethnologists, and others have shown that the Negritos are the surviving remnant of the slaves brought to our islands by the Moros in the eleventh and subsequent centuries. They are not especially negroid in appearance, and only those inhabiting the Province of Bataan in Luzon have curly hair.

In the large and only partially explored island of Mindanao there are several Indonesian "tribes," the chief of which are the Subanos, estimated to number from fifty to seventy thousand; the Mendayas, who are estimated to number thirty-five thousand; and the Tagabauas, comprising about thirty thousand. The Mendayas and the Manobos are said to practice, the one human sacrifice, and the other ceremonial cannibalism. But the evidence of this is conflicting and untrustworthy. It is also said that the small "tribe" of four thousand Ilongotes in Luzon are

Sixto Lopez, *The "Tribes" in the Philippines* (Boston: The New England Anti-imperialist League, 1900), 3–6, 8.

head-hunters. This has been denied and asserted on equally untrust-worthy authority. I have never met or heard of any one who had wit-nessed any of these practices. The information has always come from a neighboring people. The idea has probably arisen by travelers having seen the heads of criminals erected on spears, just as one might have witnessed the same thing a century or two ago on Temple Bar[1] or Lon-don Bridge. But if that proved head-hunting on the part of the Ilongotes, it also proves that the English people were head-hunters.

If, however, these statements are true, they are paralleled by the scalp-hunting Indians of the United States, and by the human sacrifices and ceremonial cannibalism of the Canadian Indians.

There are also the Moros of Mindanao and the Sulus. They are of course Mohammedans, and some of their institutions are contrary to the true ideals of morality and liberty.

There are a few natives on Mindoro who have not been Christianized nor tyrannized by Spain. But they have a religion and a code of morals of their own, the latter of which they adhere to and which in many respects is superior to that practised by the Spaniards. They believe in one God and are monogamists. They are a moral and hospitable people who do their duty to their fellow man, worship God in their own way, and do not believe in any kind or form of devil.

The so-called wild men of Luzon are the Igorrotes, who are "a warlike but semi-civilized people, living in villages, owning farms and cattle, irri-gating their rice fields, mining and working gold and copper and forging swords and spear heads of iron," but who have never been converted to Christianity or subdued by Spain. They are, however, prepared to submit to and recognize Aguinaldo's government[2] and have sent him presents of gold dust to assist in the war. . . .

Let us now glance very briefly at the remaining millions of Filipinos, who are generally regarded as belonging to the Malayan race.

They constitute more than nineteen-twentieths of the entire population of the Archipelago, and are divided into provincial districts, inhabited by the Visayans, the Tagalogs, the Bicols, the Ilocanos, the Pangasinans, the Pampangans, and the Cagayans. All of these provincial people belong to one race and all of them are Christian people practising the morals

---

[1]A gateway to the City of London.

[2]Emilio Aguinaldo was the president of the First Philippine Republic, established in January 1899.

and arts of civilization, and speaking dialects which are as similar to each other as are the dialects of the different provinces in England. The divergence between these dialects is much less than that between the Spanish and the Italian languages. I have travelled alone in Italy; I do not know Italian; but I have had no difficulty in understanding and in making myself understood by the Italians. Similarly, I have travelled in the Visayas and elsewhere in the Philippines and have had very much less difficulty in communicating with the Visayans and the Bicols. A Tagalog will become proficient in the Visayan or other dialects within a fortnight, and vice versa.

As a matter of fact, the difference between the dialects of the seven provincial districts would not be a real difficulty to independent self-government. First, because the difference is so slight, and secondly, because Spanish is the official language of our country, spoken by the educated people of all provinces. . . .

But if the language were a difficulty under Filipino rule it would be a still greater difficulty under American rule, due to the necessity of the introduction of English, which would form a third language in our islands. . . .

Now as to the supposed enmity between the so-called "tribes." Such enmity is quite unknown among our people. There may be, and no doubt there is, enmity between individuals, but the enmity does not exist between the so-called "tribes" or provinces. During the short term when our government was not interfered with the most perfect harmony and unanimity existed, and provincial and racial differences were never even thought of. . . .

As a matter of fact, with the exception of the few uncivilized tribes in central Mindanao and the Sulus, and the semi-civilized Igorrotes and Negritos of Luzon to which I have referred, the Filipinos are a homogeneous people belonging to the Malayan race. They speak several dialects, but they are *one* people. They constitute an overwhelming majority of the inhabitants of the Philippines. They are opposed not solely to American but to any foreign rule; and they are united in the desire for independence and for the purpose of maintaining a stable, independent government.

41

DAVID P. BARROWS

If Possible Take the Following Six Measurements
1901

The Bureau of Non-Christian Tribes for the Philippine Islands was established under the Department of the Interior in 1901. Its charge, to study the non-Christian peoples of the Philippines and recommend legislation "in behalf of these uncivilized peoples," resembled the duties of the Bureau of Ethnology, a research arm of the Smithsonian established by Congress to study North American Indians. Indeed, Congress called on the Bureau of Non-Christian Tribes to "affiliate its efforts" with those of the U.S. Bureau of Indian Affairs. David P. Barrows had done extensive anthropological field research among Native Americans before becoming chief of the Bureau of Non-Christian Tribes.

To those able to make an exhaustive study of any tribe, a detailed syllabus of investigation which is under preparation will be sent as soon as printed. For the investigator of fewer opportunities the following suggestions for observations are made:

1. Learn carefully the names of the tribe. . . .

2. Study and describe the habitat or territory occupied by the tribe. . . .

3. Although physical anthropology can be pursued with the best results only by following precise rules and making exact measurements with instruments, yet physical data of much value can be gained by careful observation. Accustom yourself to notice physical features so as to gradually form in your own mind a correct description of the prevalent type. Notice color of the skin both on exposed and unexposed portions of the body; color of hair and eyes; character of hair, whether fine, coarse, straight,

---

David P. Barrows, *The Bureau of Non-Christian Tribes for the Philippine Islands, Circular of Information, Instructions for Volunteer Field Workers* (Manila: Museum of Ethnology, Natural History and Commerce, 1901), 9–11.

wavy, wooly, or growing in little spiral kinks peculiar to the negro. Is the eye large and wide open or is it narrow with slanting or folding lid (mongoloid character)? Notice the muscular structure; are the limbs and body plump and rounded with full cheeks, or is the frame loose, flesh thin and cheeks sunken? Is there a well developed calf to the leg, or does this muscle seem to be small and atrophied so that the heel bone projects backward? Are there unusual deposits of fat or adipose tissue in the body especially about the hips and buttocks? Are the breasts of women long and pendent or rounded and erect? Does the hair readily turn gray? Does baldness occur? Note carefully the distribution and comparative abundance of the hair on the face. Does it grow low on the brow and is there, in addition, a fine growth distributed over the forehead? Are the teeth perfect?

If possible take the following . . . measurements: (1) stature in bare feet; (2) "grande envergure," or the extreme distance between the tips of the middle fingers when the arms are held straight out from the body; in other words the maximum reach of the arms and hands. This will ordinarily fall a little below the stature, but in the case of the Negritos it is always *more* than the stature. . . .

From the measurements on the head we obtain the "cephalic index" by multiplying the breadth by 100 and dividing by the length. The result gives us a

long head, dolichocephalic......................	64 to 69
sub-dolichocephalic................	70 to 74
medium head, mesaticephalic.................	75 to 79
sub-brachycephalic................	80 to 84
or a short head, brachycephalic..............	80 to 90

The cephalic index is of a good deal of importance in Anthropology. In a general way much variation in the index of different individuals of a tribe denotes the mixture of two or more different elements. The Malay race is brachycephalic, index 75 to 85, and the Negrito is very brachycephalic, in some recorded cases exceeding 96.

Similarly from the nasal breadth and length, we get the nasal index upon the living with the following nomenclature:

leptorhinian, long thin noses...................	below 69
mesorhinian, medium noses...................	69 to 81
platyrhinian, flat, wide noses...................	above 81

This is one of the most significant and important characters in physical anthropology. Its results always hold good more nearly than any other. In a general way all the white races and peoples are leptorhinian, the yellow or Asiatic, including the American Indians, mesorhinian, and the black race, Australian, Melanesian, and African, platyrhinian.

42

LOUIS S. MEIKLE

With the Americans You Must Be White!

1912

Most of the workers who constructed the Panama Canal hailed from Jamaica and Barbados. Like African American canal workers, they were paid in silver pesos. Construction officials reserved most of the skilled and managerial positions for white U.S. and European workers, paid in gold coins. Since silver coins were not redeemable in gold-only establishments, the dual currency system helped establish racial segregation in the U.S.-governed Canal Zone. A Jamaican in origin, Louis S. Meikle studied medicine at Howard University in Washington, D.C. He later worked as a medical corps inspector in the Panama Canal Zone. Claims that only U.S. intervention would save Jamaica from a Haitian-style revolution pitting poor black Jamaicans against the white colonial elite prompted him to write the book from which this selection was taken.

There are so many objections to advance against the annexation of the British West Indian possessions to the United States that the commercial benefits which would be derived from such a union are completely overshadowed.

One of the main points at issue is the standard of inequality (set up by the Americans with respect to other persons) based on colour, creed, and race, irrespective of qualifications.

Louis S. Meikle, *Confederation of the British West Indies versus Annexation to the United States of America* (London: Sampson Low, Marston and Co., 1912), 43–44, 62–63, 65, 92.

With the Americans you must be White! White!! White!!! You must be white to be truthful and honest. You must be white to hold any position of trust outside of the political realm; and more than all, the American white man is rated, in the United States, at a higher premium than any other member of the Caucasian race, and so it is wherever the Stars and Stripes float as the controlling power.

In this connection, with reference to race hatred, it is not the negro alone that is singled out for attack. The Jews, the Chinese, and the Japanese come in for their proportionate share of ostracism, with the exception that it is administered to these in a much milder form. . . .

Let the annexationists take a trip to Puerto Rico, Cuba, or the Philippines, and last, but not least, the Republic of Panama, and see for themselves how these people are being treated by the Americans, before attempting to barter their birthright for a mere shadow.

It is safe to say that the experience of the inquirer would be of such an astounding nature as to compel him to abandon his unrighteous cause for all time.

On the Isthmus of Panama, where, like the West Indies, the larger portion of the population is either mixed with negro or Indian blood, the expected has happened. Americans from the Canal Zone who go over to the cities of Panama and Colon, on the territory of Panama, to make small purchases (the large purchases being procured from the U.S. Commissary) are now refusing to be attended to by coloured clerks, and as a result, managers and owners of these establishments have been contemplating whether, for the benefit of their business, they should not dispense with coloured help altogether.

There is great and widespread unrest in Cuba and Panama over the extreme position taken up by the Americans, who have assumed the position of official masters.

These people have made themselves overbearing in their manner to such an extent towards every one with whom they come in contact, that they foster hatred rather than love, to their discredit as juvenile colonizers.

The Republic of Panama, having practically surrendered their sovereignty to the United States in a most extraordinary document called the "Panama Canal Treaty," which gives the latter the power of eminent domain in perpetuity, are now in a quandary what to do with the Americans who have unblushingly taken unto themselves the role of dictators over their country. . . .

No sooner had the United States implanted herself on the Isthmus of Panama, than the Americans began to set up their *religion*, that the superiority of one man over the other was not dependent upon education, achievement, or wealth, but upon the hue of the skin.

At the restaurants and boarding-houses a screen would be put before the table of a previously welcomed coloured patron, and *that table* removed to the rear of the dining-room: then he would be asked to use the side entrance there-after.

Since the advent of the Americans on the Isthmus, bar-rooms, ice-cream parlours, billiard parlours, and other places of refreshment and amusement which were opened to every one, now admit only white persons.

Those who travelled in Cuba returned with a tale of woe, that the same intolerable conditions exist there which were unknown in the darkest days of Spain's regime; and the reason for this state of affairs is attributed to Yankee invasion.

It has been argued that the American Constitution does not follow the flag: that may be so, but it is a certainty that the feeling of race-hatred follows the people wherever they go. . . .

The inhabitants of Puerto Rico, Cuba, and Panama, would gladly return to their former control, rather than tolerate for another day the dictates which come with American rule, but it is *too late! too late!!*

43

J. J. [JUAN JOSÉ] OSUNA

An Indian in Spite of Myself

1932

Prior to the U.S. landing, Puerto Rico had the highest illiteracy rates in the West Indies, with about 83 percent of its population unschooled. The Spanish colonial government established a secondary school system only in 1882. Since there was no university on the island, students seeking a postsecondary education traveled to Spain, France, or the United States. J. J. Osuna was among the Puerto Rican students sent by colonial officials to the Carlisle Indian Industrial School, a boarding school founded in

J. J. Osuna, "An Indian in Spite of Myself," *Summer School Review* 10 (1932): 2–4. Juan José Osuna Papers, 1905–1977, Box 2: Publications. Reprinted by permission of James Osuna.

1879 to assimilate Native American children into Euro-American ways through separation from their families and communities; military-style discipline; academic, religious, and industrial education; and labor. (See Document 10.)

One day in October, 1900, my employer, Don Quintiliano Cádiz, manager of Solá, Cádiz & Cía., a tobacco corporation of Caguas, Puerto Rico, asked me if I would like to go to the United States to be educated....

My mother half acquiesced to my going; Don Quintiliana put me in a buggy and we started for San Juan.... Soon we reached the heart of the city; and, after putting up our buggy, we walked to *La Plaza de Armas*, entered a building, and went up several flights of stairs which led us into a very high room. Here, fitting into the hugeness of things as they appeared to me, stood a big, tall *americano*. The gentleman was Dr. Martin G. Brumbaugh, first Commissioner of Education in Puerto Rico, appointed by President McKinley. This tall man put his large hands on my small thin shoulders, turned me around, looked me up and down—which was not very far—and then talked quite a bit with Don Quintiliano. Although I knew no English, I surmised that my case was being considered sympathetically, for the Commissioner seemed pleased with my diminutive self. I was informed that the United States government was going to send a group of bright girls and boys from the Island to be educated for a profession in American schools. In spite of the fact that I was not attending school then, the Commissioner, after the personal interview and upon the recommendation of my friend, decided that I could be included in the group....

... On the morning of the 26th of April, after making a few small purchases for me, Don Quintiliano took me to the dock where I boarded the ship on which we were to sail, a war transport, loaded with returning soldiers, mules, horses, war implements....

No sooner had we left the harbor than a sergeant came around with a little whip, striking our bare legs in order to herd us children together. There were twenty-nine boys and one girl....

On May 1st we arrived in New York harbor. It was a cold and foggy afternoon, one of these raw spring days of lower Manhattan. No provision had been made for warm clothing. ... I stood on deck looking at the Statue of Liberty and the skyline of New York, shivering in my flimsy tropical outfit. Anyone who has experienced the temperature of New York harbor can understand how cold I must have been. The boat docked, and there stood our little company looking into the "promised land," wondering what it had in store for us. . . .

The next day we arrived at a town where we boarded a street car. The trolley traveled a few miles; it stopped; and we were told that we had arrived at our destination. It was six o'clock in the morning. Each of us was carrying his small baggage as we entered the campus.

We looked at the windows of the buildings, and very peculiar-looking faces peered out at us. We had never seen such people before. The buildings seemed full of them. Behold, we had arrived at the Carlisle Indian School! The United States of America, our new rulers, thought that the people of Puerto Rico were Indians; hence they should be sent to an Indian school, and Carlisle happened to be the nearest.

Our lives as Indians began May 2nd, 1901, at six o'clock in the morning. I was assigned to the small boys quarters. Mother Given had me take a bath, and she gave me the school uniform. It felt good to be dressed in warm woolen clothes. The first and second days we were allowed to roam around the grounds, but soon we came under the rigorous discipline of the school. By the second day we had received our working outfit: overalls, checkered shirts, and heavy shoes. . . .

Among the many experiences in Carlisle, those connected with the industrial work were most interesting. All the large boys had to choose a trade, while we smaller ones were assigned all sorts of duties from house-cleaning to serving as orderly to General Pratt, the founder and at that time the Superintendent of the School. One day, two or three hundred of us were set to work weeding a large onion field. We were strung out in a long line with task-master Bennett, the farmer, keeping the line of progress as straight as he could by the aid of a whip, which he used freely when any one lagged behind. I always managed to keep a bit ahead of the main line. However, this type of education was not exactly in keeping with my preconceived ideas of the "land of promise."

I worked there for the summer and went to school during the academic year of 1901–1902. Of the rest of my companions, some stayed like myself to work and study; some ran away and returned to Puerto Rico; and the parents of the well-to-do either sent for their children or transferred them to other schools. We were a very disappointed lot. I had decided to become a lawyer, but I did not see that in this school I would ever get nearer my goal. Nevertheless, I continued studying and learned what I could. I was handicapped by not knowing English. We spoke Spanish to each other constantly, and therefore made but little progress in our new language.

It was the custom at Carlisle to place the boys and girls in country homes all over Pennsylvania during the summer. The children would generally return in the fall. . . .

Leaving Bloomsburg in a milk wagon, I arrived at the farm [in Orangeville] March 28, 1902. . . . My new employers were Scotch-Irish, and of the most puritanic, blue stocking type. . . . I was a curiosity in the neighborhood. That particular section was made up of old families who had settled there in the early history of the state. They had kept all foreigners out. Once in a while a Jewish peddler would come around and, of course, he was looked upon with suspicion. As far as I know, I was the first foreigner to be allowed to live in this community. Perhaps my success at establishing myself here was due to the fact that I went there as an aboriginal American.

As I was different from the Indians, and also somewhat different from the Americans, I became a curiosity. On Sunday afternoons, the place was visited by people from all over that section of the country who came purposely to see Miss Mira's new boy. They had heard that he was not an Indian, that he had come from Puerto Rico; and they wanted to see what Puerto Ricans looked like.

Instead of returning in the fall of 1902 to Carlisle, I remained with my employer and went to a rural school. I did not want to return to Carlisle. Frankly, I did not like the place. I never thought it was the school for me. I was not an Indian; I was a Puerto Rican of Spanish descent. However, I was a student of the Federal Government, supposed to be located at Carlisle, but with permission to stay at Orangeville, Pennsylvania. . . .

In the spring of 1905, I received a letter reminding me that I was still a Carlisle student, but that the authorities felt that I was advanced enough to graduate from the institution and sever my relations with the Federal Government. I was furthermore informed that the Government would pay my railroad fare to Carlisle and back, that I would be supplied with two suits of clothes, shoes, and all sorts of wearing apparel, if I desired to go to Carlisle and graduate. At the time I was working my way through Bloomsburg Normal and had very little of anything that I could call my own. I naturally accepted the proposition. I went to Carlisle, attended commencement, and received all that had been promised me in the way of this world's goods. Moreover, I received a diploma of the Carlisle Indian Industrial School. I graduated with the class of 1905; I am an alumnus of the Carlisle Indian Industrial School. I am an Indian in spite of myself.

9

Commercial Interests

44

IDA B. WELLS-BARNETT

Opportunities in Africa
1892

The end of Reconstruction reignited the African colonization movement. Although the American Colonization Society helped relocate only a handful of emigrants a year in the 1890s, the back-to-Africa movement caught the imaginations of poor black farmers in the South, who saw in Africa the prospect of land ownership and an escape from white supremacy. As in the pre–Civil War period, such sentiments sparked opposition from other African Americans. Among their objections was that Africa offered no escape from white supremacy, given European imperialism. Ida B. Wells-Barnett's anti-lynching activism made her one of the most prominent civil rights advocates of her day. She helped found the National Association for Colored Women in 1896 and the National Association for the Advancement of Colored People in 1909.

The object of this paper is to maintain that the right of those who wish to go to Africa should be as inviolate as that of those who wish to stay. That there are Afro-Americans who would return to Africa is proved by the presence in New York City last winter of three hundred who had managed to get that far in their journey. Somebody had told them they

Ida B. Wells-Barnett, "Afro-Americans and Africa," *A.M.E. Church Review* 9 (July 1892): 41–43.

would be carried free if they got to New York. They were of course disappointed and returned to the South. The mistake these people made was not in wanting to go to Africa, but in being so poorly prepared in intelligence and finance. There are hundreds of others besides these poverty-stricken and ignorant people, all over the country, who chafe under the knowledge that what is the opportunity for the European and Chinese emigrant in this country is his disadvantage. In no other country but the vaunted "land of the free and home of the brave" is a man despised because of his color. As the Irish, Swede, Dutch, Italian and other foreigners find this the "sweet land of liberty," the Afro-American finds it the land of oppression, outrage and persecution. In the freest and most unprejudiced sections, in every walk of life, no matter how well dressed, courteous or intellectual, he never knows when he may not meet with and be humiliated by this distinctively American prejudice. He is becoming restless and discontented. He wishes to enjoy the full freedom of manhood and aspiration. Where shall he go?

Why should not they turn to Africa, the land of their forefathers, the most fertile of its kind, and the only one which the rapacious and ubiquitous Anglo-Saxon has not entirely gobbled—where they would be welcomed by their race, and given opportunities to assist in the development of Africa, such as are not possessed by any other nation waiting for a foothold?

That more Afro-Americans do not go to Africa is because the objectors say Africa is a death-trap, that we are not Africans, and that it is a country "without organized government, accepted religion or uniform language."

Everybody who goes to Africa does not die. Everybody knows of the African or acclimating fevers, and all travelers or explorers agree that with care and attention to diet, changes of weather and care of the system, the African fever is no more deadly than our Southern malaria; yet nobody thinks of staying away from the South because of it. The cause of death-rate is carelessness rather than the fever. All writers again agree that it is only along the low, marshy coast that this prevails. Back in the interior it is more healthy. . . .

The argument that Afro-Americans should not go to Africa because "it is a country without organized government, accepted religion or uniform language," is the very weakest that could be offered. No better reinforcement of the position of southern whites could be deduced than to concede the Afro-American incapable of self-government or the government of others. Children, or inherently weak persons, wait for the path to be blazed out in which they should walk. The Romans who invaded Britain, nor yet the Puritans who came over in the "Mayflower," waited for "organized government, uniform language, or established religion." They brought their own customs, language and religion with them, few in number though they were, and engrafted them into the warp and woof of the body politic. Is the Afro-American incapable of doing this?

It may be argued that it is not the intelligent class who wish to go to Africa. If this is true it is discreditable alike to their intelligence and desire for gain that they do not. The resources of Africa are boundless. White men of every nationality are braving "the white man's grave," and growing rich off the simple natives. They go home every three years to recover health, then go back to the work of making a fortune. They endure all things in their young manhood for the hope of affluence in their declining years. And if they die, as die they do, will not their children reap the benefit? . . .

What a grand opportunity for the many wealthy colored men in our country! They could build ships and grow wealthy off the trade, or they could form a syndicate and transport and maintain those who will go, and whose brawn and muscle will assist in the development of the country and the greater increase of wealth to themselves.

45

THEODORE ROOSEVELT

Placing the Customhouses beyond the Temptation of Insurgent Chieftains

1905

In 1899, the Dominican Republic entered a period of instability following the assassination of its dictator, Ulises Heureaux. In addition to weighing calls for intervention from U.S. investors, President Theodore Roosevelt grappled with concerns that European powers would send in troops to

"President Roosevelt on Santo Domingo. Message Sent to the Senate," *Boston Daily Globe*, February 17, 1905, 11.

enforce payment of the debts due to their citizens. In January 1905, Roosevelt signed a protocol giving the U.S. government control of Dominican customhouses (the main sources of government revenue). He sent the following message to the U.S. Senate along with the agreement.

To the Senate—I submit herewith a protocol concluded between the Dominican republic and the United States.

The conditions in the republic of Santo Domingo have been growing steadily worse for many years. There have been many disturbances and revolutions, and debts have been contracted beyond the power of the republic to pay. Some of these debts were properly contracted and are held by those who have a legitimate right to their money. Others are without question improper or exorbitant, constituting claims which should never be paid in full, and perhaps only to the extent of a very small portion of their nominal value.

Certain foreign countries have long felt themselves aggrieved because of the nonpayment of debts due their citizens. The only way by which foreign creditors could ever obtain from the republic itself any guaranty of payment would be either by the acquisition of territory outright or temporarily, or else by taking possession of the customhouses, which would of course in itself in effect be taking possession of a certain amount of territory.

It has for some time been obvious that those who profit by the Monroe doctrine must accept certain responsibilities along with the rights which it confers; and that the same statement applies to those who uphold the doctrine. It cannot be too often and too emphatically asserted that the United States has not the slightest desire for territorial aggrandizement at the expense of any of its southern neighbors, and will not treat the Monroe doctrine as an excuse for such aggrandizement on its part.

We do not propose to take any part of Santo Domingo or exercise any other control over the island save what is necessary to its financial rehabilitation in connection with the collection of revenue, part of which will be turned over to the government to meet the necessary expense of running it, and part of which will be distributed pro rata among the creditors of the republic upon a basis of absolute equality.

The justification for the United States taking this burden and incurring this responsibility is to be found in the fact that it is incompatible with international equity for the United States to refuse to allow other powers to take the only means at their disposal of satisfying the claims of their creditors and yet to refuse itself to take any such steps. . . .

Under the accepted law of nations, foreign governments are within their right, if they choose to exercise it, when they actively intervene in support of the contractual claims of their subjects.

They sometimes exercise this power, and on account of commercial rivalries there is a growing tendency on the part of other governments more and more to aid diplomatically in the enforcement of the claims of their subjects.

In view of the dilemma in which the government of the United States is thus placed, it must either adhere to its usual attitude of nonintervention in such cases—an attitude proper under normal conditions, but one which in this particular kind of case results to the disadvantage of its citizens in comparison with those of other states—or else it must, in order to be consistent in its policy, actively intervene to protect the contracts and concessions of its citizens engaged in agriculture, commerce and transportation in competition with the subjects and citizens of other states. . . .

As the result of chronic disorders attended with a constant increase of debt, the state of things in Santo Domingo has become hopeless, unless the United States or some other strong government shall interpose to bring order out of the chaos.

The customhouses, with the exception of the two in the possession of the financial agent appointed by the United States, have become unproductive for the discharge of indebtedness, except as to persons making emergency loans to the government or to its enemies for the purpose of carrying on political contests by force. They have, in fact, become the nuclei of the various revolutions.

The first effort of revolutionists is to take possession of a customhouse so as to obtain funds, which are then disposed of at the absolute discretion of those who are collecting them.

The chronic disorders prevailing in Santo Domingo have, moreover, become exceedingly dangerous to the interests of Americans holding property in that country.

Constant complaints have been received of the injuries and inconveniences to which they have been subjected. As an evidence of the increasing aggravation of conditions, the fact may be mentioned that about a year ago the American railway, which had previously been exempt from such attacks, was seized, its tracks torn up and a station destroyed by revolutionary bands.

The ordinary resources of diplomacy and international arbitration are absolutely impotent to deal wisely and effectively with the situation in the Dominican republic, which can only be met by organizing its finances on a sound basis and by placing the customhouses beyond the temptation of insurgent chieftains. . . .

We can point with just pride to what we have done in Cuba as a guaranty of our good faith. We stayed in Cuba only so long as to start her aright on the road to self-government, which she has since trod with such marked and distinguished success; and upon leaving the island we exacted no conditions, save such as would prevent her from ever becoming the prey of the stranger.

Our purpose in Santo Domingo is as beneficent. The good that this country got from its action in Cuba was indirect rather than direct. So it is as regards Santo Domingo. The chief material advantage that will come from the action proposed to be taken will be to Santo Domingo itself and to Santo Domingo's creditors.

The advantage that will come to the United States will be indirect, but nevertheless great, for it is supremely to our interest that all communities immediately south of us should be or become prosperous and stable, and therefore not merely in name, but in fact, independent and self-governing.

46

WILLIAM ENGLISH CARSON

The United States Has about $750,000,000 Invested in Mexico

1909

Hoping to modernize his country, the long-serving Mexican president Porfirio Díaz (in power 1876–1911) encouraged U.S. investment. As a result, U.S. banks, railroads, and mining companies expanded their operations in Mexico, as did ranchers, sugar producers, and growers of henequen (a fiber used mainly in twine). Supervisors from the United States earned twenty times that of Mexican laborers in the mining industry; on plantations, the earnings ratio was 30:1. The U.S. business

W. E. Carson, "The Foreign Invasion," in *Mexico: The Wonderland of the South* (New York: Macmillan, 1909), 170–71, 173–76.

presence in Mexico fueled not only anti-yanqui sentiment but also opposition to Díaz, whose regime ended in the Mexican Revolution. William English Carson, a New York–based newspaper correspondent, wrote this account after a tour through Mexico.

Mexicans being naturally averse to all business enterprise or energetic action, have for years past left the development of their country to the strangers within their gates. Unless he is a man of wealth, the Mexican usually has one ambition, and that is to become a government employee. With this satisfied, he cares little about banking, trading or mining; at any rate, he does not care enough about them to put himself out and work hard. Thus it is that while the foreigners in Mexico form a comparatively small percentage of the population, yet their importance is not to be reckoned by mere numbers.

The English-speaking population of Mexico City is about six thousand, of which a very large proportion are Americans. What is true of the capital is also true of the country at large, and throughout Mexico there are more Americans than any other foreign nationality. Within the past decade they have been simply swarming in, and with them have come millions of dollars of American money, which Mexico is destined to find a serious factor some day. Formerly, Americans were engaged simply in mining and railway building, but to-day they are to be found in nearly every branch of commerce. In Mexico City one sees American banks, and agencies for all kinds of American goods, such as sewing-machines, typewriters and agricultural machinery; there are American grocers, druggists, booksellers and fancy goods stores, also tailors, hotels and restaurants. So large a number of Americans are collected in the capital that there is an extensive American quarter, where there are modern houses and flats, an American club and several American churches.

During the winter season several of our railway companies advertise Mexico extensively as a winter paradise. They give away tens of thousands of beautifully illustrated booklets describing the wonders of the land. They run cheap excursion trains to Mexico and bring down thousands of sight-seeing tourists, most of whom come from the Western states. The newspapers in Mexico City publish, every day, lists of people stopping at the various hotels. I noticed that the American visitors usually came from such places as Kalamazoo, Mich., Tombstone, Arizona, Cross Roads, Iowa, or Jaytown City, Neb. To most of these people Mexico must certainly seem a land of wonders; they have never been in Europe, and for the first time in their lives they see old churches, cathedrals and ruins, and mingle among people who have a different language and strange customs. . . .

One very gratifying feature of life in Mexico is the thoroughly good feeling which exists between Englishmen and Americans resident in the Republic. The ties of language and race seem to draw them together. Not only are they associated very closely in business but also in the social life of the country. In most of the American clubs Englishmen and Canadians are also eligible for membership, and the fraternal feeling which exists between the three branches of the English-speaking world shows that no paper treaty is needed to bring them into alliance. . . .

Most Americans have a firm impression that Mexicans love the United States and that ill-will towards us has practically disappeared. Impartial observers have, however, assured me that a strong anti-American feeling exists in some quarters, for which there are several reasons. In the first place, many Americans in Mexico are much given to boasting that American capital is getting control of all the best mines and otherwise acquiring a great hold on the country. To this is added the bragging of the low-class American—only too common in Mexico—who calls the Mexican "a greaser," and is always asserting that a few hundred Americans could beat the Mexican army and conquer the land.

An American resident told me that while he was lunching one day in a Mexico City restaurant, he heard a party of Westerners discussing the country in very uncomplimentary terms. One of them seemed to be interested in a mining company, which he thought had been unjustly treated by the Mexican government. "If these d—d greasers don't let up on this sort of thing," he said, "we Americans will have to teach them another lesson. Why, man, we could march a few regiments down here from Texas alone, and whip the everlasting stuffing out of them." At a neighboring table sat some young Mexicans, two of them sons of cabinet ministers, and all understanding English perfectly. From their looks they did not seem to exactly relish the American's remarks. . . .

All attempts of Mexicans to halt the onward march of progress are, however, certain to end in failure. Whether Mexicans like it or not, every year is witnessing a more pronounced Americanization of Mexico, more American settlers are pouring into the country than ever before, and in two more decades their numbers and influence will be formidable. With the increasing use of the English language among the people, and the education of the masses, old prejudices are gradually disappearing, and the commercial and social ties between Americans and Mexicans are steadily drawing them closer. It is never safe to prophesy unless you know; but it would not be so strange if, under these conditions, an

Americanized Mexico should some day—perhaps in twenty-five years, or so—become peacefully annexed to the United States.

47

WILLIAM T. HORNADAY

All That Remained of Them Were Several Acres of Bones
1913

Guano *is the term for bird excrement, which is of great value as a fertilizer. According to the terms of the 1856 Guano Islands Act, American citizens could claim uninhabited islands with guano deposits. Under this legislation, U.S. citizens claimed dozens of islands in the Caribbean, Pacific, Atlantic, and Indian oceans. They proceeded to mine the droppings with gangs of workers, many of them brought to the islands by fraud or force. The guano gone, the United States kept some of the islands for lighthouses, meteorological and radio stations, and, by World War II, landing strips. Laysan is a small island in the Hawai'ian island chain. Zoologist William T. Hornaday included this account in a volume on wildlife depletion.*

Ever since 1891 the bird life on Laysan has been regarded as one of the wonders of the bird world. One of the photographs taken prior to 1909 shows a vast plain, apparently a square mile in area, covered and crowded with Laysan albatrosses. They stand there on the level sand, serene, bulky and immaculate. Thousands of birds appear in one view—a very remarkable sight.

Naturally man, the ever-greedy, began to cast about for ways by which to convert some product of that feathered host into money. At first guano and eggs were collected. A tramway was laid down and small box-cars were introduced, in which the collected material was piled and pushed down to the packing place.

William T. Hornaday, *Our Vanishing Wild Life: Its Extermination and Preservation* (New York: New York Zoological Society, 1913), 137–42. Reprinted in 1970 by Arno Press.

For several years this went on, and the birds themselves were not molested. At last, however, a tentacle of the feather-trade octopus reached out to Laysan. In an evil moment in the spring of 1909, a predatory individual of Honolulu and elsewhere, named Max Schlemmer, decided that the wings of those albatross, gulls and terns should be torn off and sent to Japan, whence they would undoubtedly be shipped to Paris, the special market for the wings of sea-birds slaughtered in the North Pacific.

Schlemmer the Slaughterer bought a cheap vessel, hired twenty-three phlegmatic and cold-blooded Japanese laborers, and organized a raid on Laysan. With the utmost secrecy he sailed from Honolulu, landed his bird-killers upon the sea-bird wonderland, and turned them loose upon the birds.

For several months they slaughtered diligently and without mercy. Apparently it was the ambition of Schlemmer to kill every bird on the island.

By the time the bird-butchers had accumulated between three and four car-loads of wings, and the carnage was half finished, William A. Bryan, Professor of Zoology in the College of Honolulu, heard of it and promptly wired the United States Government.

Without the loss of a moment the Secretary of the Navy despatched the revenue cutter *Thetis* to the shambles of Laysan. When Captain Jacobs arrived he found that in round numbers about *three hundred thousand* birds had been destroyed, and all that remained of them were several acres of bones and dead bodies, and about three carloads of wings, feathers and skins. It was evident that Schlemmer's intention was to kill all the birds on the island, and only the timely arrival of the *Thetis* frustrated that bloody plan.

The twenty-three Japanese poachers were arrested and taken to Honolulu for trial, and the *Thetis* also brought away all the stolen wings and plumage with exception of one shedful of wings that had to be left behind on account of carrying space. . . .

Three hundred thousand albatrosses, gulls, terns and other birds were butchered to make a Schlemmer holiday! Had the arrival of the *Thetis* been delayed, it is reasonably certain that every bird on Laysan would have been killed to satisfy the wolfish rapacity of one money-grubbing white man. . . .

But the work of the Evil Genius of Laysan did not stop with the slaughter of three hundred thousand birds. Mr. Schlemmer introduced rabbits and guinea-pigs; and these rapidly multiplying rodents now are threatening to consume every plant on the island. If the plants disappear, many of the insects will go with them; and this will mean the disappearance of the small insectivorous birds.

In February, 1909, President Roosevelt issued an executive order creating the Hawaiian Islands Reservation for Birds. In this are included Laysan and twelve other islands and reefs, some of which are inhabited by birds that are well worth preserving. By this act, we may feel that for the future the birds of Laysan and neighboring islets are secure from further attacks by the bloody-handed agents of the vain women who still insist upon wearing the wings and feathers of wild birds.

48

FREDERICK UPHAM ADAMS

The United Fruit Company Is More Than a Corporation

1914

Frederick Upham Adams's assertion that the United Fruit Company was "more than a corporation" took on meanings he did not anticipate: Across Latin America and the Caribbean, the company became a symbol of the inordinate power of foreign capital. Its critics denounced it for harsh labor practices, claiming that under each of its railroad ties in Costa Rica lay the body of a colored man who had died laying track. Critics also condemned the company's influence over national governments; its collaborations with exploitative local elites; its control of credit, supplies, transportation, and trade; and its massive landholdings in Panama, Costa Rica, Honduras, and Guatemala.

The banana, as an article of import and consumption in the United States, is purely a product of what I designate as the Machine. Jefferson and Franklin never had a chance to eat a banana. There did not then exist the machinery of production and distribution by which it was possible to raise bananas in commercial quantities in the tropics and transport them to Philadelphia, New York, and Boston and deliver them to

Frederick Upham Adams, *Conquest of the Tropics: The Story of the Creative Enterprises Conducted by the United Fruit Company, Romance of Big Business*, vol. 1 (Garden City, N.Y.: Doubleday, Page, 1914), 15–16, 279–81, 306, 356.

our ancestors in an edible condition. Bananas might as well have been solely a product of Mars so far as the people of the temperate zones were concerned.

The masses of the people who lived in the United States in 1870 were as unfamiliar with bananas as they were with electric lights and automobiles. It was known to them that bananas grew in the tropics, but the Machine had not yet been constructed which commercially merged New York, Chicago, and San Francisco with the fertile valleys of Costa Rica and Colombia. If a famine had occurred in the United States in the years prior to the birth of the Age of Invention, it would have been practically impossible to have levied on the fruits of the tropics. . . .

It was not until 1913 that the United Fruit Company began the planting of bananas on a large scale in Honduras. This country has been a large producer of this fruit for years, but most of it is grown by the natives, the various importing companies bidding for this product.

When the United Fruit Company decided to make the attempt to become a banana producer in Honduras it acquired a tract of land bounded by the Colorado River to the east and the Ullola River to the west, and extending back into the foothills of the Montanas de Poco (the Little Mountains). . . . The port of the new district is Tela (pronounced as if it were "Tailer"), a town of 2,000 inhabitants. . . .

Tela has a fine location both from a commercial and sanitary consideration. There is deep water and good harbor possibilities. The town lies well above the Caribbean, has natural drainage and an easily available water supply. It is open to the direct winds which ever sweep in from the sea, and has many other advantages as administrative and medical headquarters. The Tela River divides the town into two parts. The Government of Honduras has granted the company certain exclusive rights on the west side of the river, and here are its railroad yards, shops, office structures, hospital, and other buildings.

Here was a chance to illustrate on a large scale what modern scientific sanitation can accomplish in what is practically a virgin tropical wilderness. The location of these plantations is in what even the most hardened natives have denounced as a pest-hole and an impossible agricultural proposition. There are prosperous banana holdings to the east and west of it, but these growers would not accept this land as a gift. What has happened?

In a period of less than a year the planting of 50,000 acres of bananas is well under way, the building of 250 miles of railroad is being rapidly pushed, temporary piers have been constructed, and the office and other structures completed — and the health of the thousands of men employed is as good as that of the average farming community in the United States. Not only has the health of these employees been preserved, but that of the surrounding community as well. How was this miracle accomplished?

The medical staff were sent out ahead and placed on the firing line. They pushed into the wilderness with forts of mosquito-proof houses. They tested the soils and the water, and applied remedies whose worth had been proved by years of experience. It was not necessary to create a new corps of medical experts, doctors, dispensers, and nurses. These were drafted from the older divisions, and there descended on the swamps and jungles of Spanish Honduras a battalion of veterans before whom the mosquito and his breed of diseases had no more chance than had the breath of the Arctic frozen these coasts.

This is how the tropics are being conquered. This is War, and it is Magnificent! It has all the dash, the brilliancy, the courage, the organization, the discipline, the generalship and the strategy of war, and it has its heroes, dead and living. And it is a fight to create and not to destroy. Man will not have accomplished his mission on earth so long as a pestilential swamp remains to menace his fellows, and those who work to transform swamps and jungles into food-producing gardens have not lived in vain. . . .

It is safe to predict that the railways in Guatemala, Honduras, Costa Rica, and Panama will be extended and become feeders of a comprehensive system which will open all of Central America to the development and progress possible under stable conditions of government. At the present time these roads are devoted almost entirely to the transportation of bananas and to the materials used by the United Fruit Company in the prosecution of its enterprises, but the time is at hand when the innumerable possibilities of these sections will be embraced by investors from all parts of the world. The triumphs of sanitation insure that new towns will be founded along the lines of new railroads, and that the millions who one day will live and prosper in these redeemed coast lands will realize that all this was made possible by the American citizens who were the pioneers in this Conquest of the Tropics. . . .

The United Fruit Company is more than a corporation. It is an institution, an American institution founded by certain of its citizens and conducted with a broadness of policy and an industrial statesmanship which lift it out of the class of mere money making and profit hunting corporations. It is doing for the American tropics and the American people what the Hudson Bay Company did for the British Empire in the frozen north of Canada. It has awakened the slumbering nations bordering on the

Caribbean with the quickening tonic of Yankee enterprise. It has proven to the world that these tropics can be converted from a harassing liability into an asset of stupendous value, and it has solved for the world the problem of transforming deadly swamps and jungles to gardens on which can be raised the food products demanded to keep pace with the ever-increasing hunger of the city-housed multitudes.

A Chronology of U.S. Imperialism in the Caribbean and the Pacific (1844–1999)

1844 The United States signs a treaty granting it extraterritorial rights in China.

1846–
1848 The United States and Mexico fight a war stemming from the U.S. annexation of Texas in 1845 and disputes over the boundary between Texas and Mexico.

1855 The U.S.-based Panama Railroad Company completes the transisthmian Panama Railroad.

1867 The United States purchases Alaska and annexes the Midway Islands.

1868–
1878 The Ten Years' War is fought for independence in Cuba.

1871 The United States conducts military action in Korea.

1878 The United States obtains rights to Pago Pago Harbor in Samoa.

1879–
1880 The Little War is fought for independence in Cuba.

1882 The Chinese Exclusion Act denies entry to Chinese workers even as U.S. missionaries continue to expand their presence in China.

1889 José Rizal forms a Philippine nationalist association called Los Indios Bravos.

1890 The U.S. Army massacres Lakota Sioux at the Battle of Wounded Knee, its last major engagement with Native Americans.

1892 Andres Bonifacio and other Filipinos form a secret society, the Katipunan, to press for independence.

1893 *January* The Missionary Party deposes Queen Lili'uokalani (also spelled Liliuokalani) of Hawai'i.

December President Grover Cleveland withdraws a proposed
Hawai'ian annexation treaty.

1895 The third war for Cuban independence begins.

1898 *February 15* The U.S. battleship *Maine* sinks in Havana Harbor.

April 25 Congress declares war against Spain. The Teller Amendment to the war resolution pledges support for Cuban independence.

May 1 Commodore George Dewey sinks the Spanish flotilla in
Manila Bay.

June 12 Filipino leader Emilio Aguinaldo declares independence.

June 20 A U.S. fleet under Captain Henry Glass takes Guam
from the Spanish officials who had been governing its indigenous
Chomorro people.

June 22 The U.S. Army lands at Daiquirí, Cuba.

July 1 U.S. forces land in the Philippines at Cavite.

July 3 The U.S. Navy defeats Spain's Caribbean naval force at
the Battle of Santiago.

July 7 A joint resolution of Congress annexes Hawai'i to the
United States.

July 17 U.S. forces occupy Santiago, Cuba, a day after the Spanish surrender.

July 21 U.S. troops invade Puerto Rico.

November The Anti-imperialist League forms in Boston.

1899 *January 17* The United States claims Wake Island and later
establishes a cable station there.

February 4 Fighting commences between U.S. troops and Filipino soldiers.

February 6 The U.S. Senate ratifies the Treaty of Paris, which
cedes the Philippines to the United States.

March–May The United States and Britain land troops in Samoa
to thwart German expansion. The great powers settle their dispute, and the United States keeps the island of Tutuila and the
naval base at Pago Pago.

**1899–
1901** Boxers attack Chinese Christians and foreign nationals in China.

1900 *April 2* The Foraker Act (also known as the Organic Act) establishes a civilian government in Puerto Rico, with a governor to be
appointed by the U.S. president.

May The United States lands troops in China as part of a multi-imperial force to put down the Boxer Uprising.

1901   *February*   Congress passes the Platt Amendment limiting Cuban independence. It is later written into a 1901 addendum to the Cuban constitution and a 1903 treaty between the United States and Cuba.

May 27   The Supreme Court rules in *Downes v. Bidwell* that Puerto Rico is a territory belonging to the United States that could be treated differently from other parts of the United States.

September 28   Filipino nationalists attack U.S. troops on the island of Samar in an event that comes to be known in the United States as the Balangiga massacre. Filipinos regard the U.S. retaliation as the real massacre of Balangiga.

1902   *May 20*   The U.S. military withdraws from Cuba.

July 4   President Theodore Roosevelt declares the war in the Philippines over, but the fighting continues.

1903   The United States acquires a ten-mile-wide strip of land in Panama to build a canal.

1904   In his corollary to the Monroe Doctrine, Roosevelt claims that the United States has the right to exercise police power in the hemisphere.

1905   The United States occupies the Dominican Republic.

1906   In the Battle of Bud Daju, Moro Province, the Philippines, an estimated six hundred Muslims die, and eighteen U.S. soldiers are killed.

1906–1909   The United States stations troops in Cuba to maintain order.

1907   The bicameral Philippine Assembly is established.

1912   The United States lands troops in Cuba to protect U.S. property.

New Mexico and Arizona become states.

The Moro Wars in the Philippines wind down.

1912–1925   The United States occupies Nicaragua.

1914   *April–November*   The United States occupies Veracruz, Mexico.

1915–1934   The United States occupies Haiti.

1916   The first Jones Act promises independence to the Philippines when a stable government has been established, as determined by the United States.

1916–1917   A punitive expedition into Mexico follows Francisco "Pancho" Villa's raid into Columbus, New Mexico.

1916–

1924   The United States occupies the Dominican Republic.

1917   The United States acquires the Danish Virgin Islands.

           The United States stations troops in Cuba.

           The second Jones Act grants U.S. citizenship to Puerto Ricans and creates a Puerto Rican legislature, subject to veto by the presidentially appointed governor.

1920   The United States lands troops in Cuba.

1934   President Franklin Roosevelt repeals the Platt Amendment but keeps the U.S. base at Guantánamo.

           The Tydings-McDuffie Act promises Philippine independence on July 4, 1946.

1941   *December 8*   Japan attacks and subsequently occupies the Philippines until the U.S. reconquest of the islands in 1944–1945.

1946   *July 4*   The Philippines gains independence from the United States.

1948   Puerto Ricans win the right to elect their own governor.

1952   Puerto Rico becomes a U.S. commonwealth.

1959   The territory of Hawaii becomes a U.S. state.

1979   The United States relinquishes jurisdiction over the ten-mile-wide Panama Canal Zone.

1999   Panama assumes complete control over the Panama Canal.

Questions for Consideration

1. How did continental expansion before 1898 resemble and differ from the Caribbean and Pacific interventions of the late nineteenth and early twentieth centuries?
2. What precedents did U.S. relations with Native Americans provide for relations with other people of color in colonial contexts?
3. How did the global imperial system of the late nineteenth and early twentieth centuries shape U.S. imperial endeavors?
4. What do these documents reveal about inter-imperial rivalries, cooperation, and connections?
5. What did the civilizing mission imply? How did it intersect with and diverge from Christianizing and Americanizing efforts?
6. Whose interests did missionaries serve?
7. Do these documents support the claim that roots of modern multiculturalism can be found among liberal Protestant missionaries?
8. If you were a Cuban, Filipino, or Puerto Rican nationalist, how would you have regarded the U.S. declaration of war against Spain and the subsequent deployment of troops to Cuba, the Philippines, and Puerto Rico?
9. How does the Platt Amendment compare to the Teller Amendment? How would you explain the differences between them? Do any common assumptions shape both documents?
10. Should the military in this period be seen as advancing democracy, whether within its ranks or more generally?
11. How did factors such as race, class, gender, region, and national origin affect perspectives on imperial issues?
12. Did the participants in debates over U.S.-Philippine policy speak *to* one another or *past* one another? Did imperialists and anti-imperialists share any common assumptions?
13. How cohesive was the anti-imperial political coalition?
14. Were those who debated U.S. imperial policy more concerned with the implications of empire for the Philippines or for the United States?

15. How patriotic were those who criticized military conduct and government policy in a time of war?

16. What do these documents reveal about the possibilities of teaching self-government?

17. How effectively did the United States carry out its goals of "benevolent assimilation" in the Philippines?

18. Should U.S. colonial governance be seen more as a model for Progressivism, as a result of Progressivism, or as a counter to Progressivism?

19. In what ways did military personnel and civilian officials draw on missionary language and visions, and how did they position themselves and their project differently?

20. The authors of these documents express a great deal of interest in "native character." What might a reader conclude about "U.S. character" based on these documents?

21. How did U.S. race relations affect understandings of racial difference in the Caribbean and Pacific, and vice versa?

22. According to U.S. imperialists, what would determine Filipinos' readiness for self-government? Do you think the United States would have qualified for self-government according to the standards they set forth?

23. Should consumers who purchased tropical goods be held accountable for environmentally destructive and exploitative business practices?

24. What do these documents reveal about the intersections between economic and political power?

25. What are some of the patterns that emerge across different sites of U.S. intervention in the Caribbean and Pacific?

26. What are some of the major changes over time revealed by these documents?

27. How did the imperial relations covered in these documents help shape the global connections of today?

28. How does attentiveness to empire change your understanding of American history?

Selected Bibliography

PATHS OF EMPIRE BEFORE 1898

Clegg, Claude A., III. *The Price of Liberty: African Americans and the Making of Liberia.* Chapel Hill: University of North Carolina Press, 2004.

Greenberg, Amy S. *A Wicked War: Polk, Clay, Lincoln, and the 1846 U.S. Invasion of Mexico.* New York: Knopf, 2012.

Hietala, Thomas R. *Manifest Design: American Exceptionalism and Empire.* Rev. ed. Ithaca, N.Y.: Cornell University Press, 2003.

Hixson, Walter L. *American Settler Colonialism: A History.* New York: Palgrave Macmillan, 2013.

McGuinness, Aims. *Path of Empire: Panama and the California Gold Rush.* Ithaca, N.Y.: Cornell University Press, 2008.

Ostler, Jeffrey. *The Plains Sioux and U.S. Colonialism from Lewis and Clark to Wounded Knee.* New York: Cambridge University Press, 2004.

Sexton, Jay. *The Monroe Doctrine: Empire and Nation in Nineteenth-Century America.* New York: Hill and Wang, 2011.

Weeks, William Earl. *Building the Continental Empire: American Expansion from the Revolution to the Civil War.* Chicago: Ivan R. Dee, 1996.

GENERAL HISTORIES OF U.S. EMPIRE AROUND 1898

Gatewood, Willard B., Jr. *Black Americans and the White Man's Burden, 1898–1903.* Urbana: University of Illinois Press, 1975.

LaFeber, Walter. *The American Search for Opportunity, 1865–1913.* Cambridge: Cambridge University Press, 1993.

———. *The New Empire: An Interpretation of American Expansionism.* Ithaca, N.Y.: Cornell University Press, 1963.

Love, Eric T. *Race over Empire: Racism and U.S. Imperialism, 1865–1900.* Chapel Hill: University of North Carolina Press, 2004.

McCoy, Alfred W., and Francisco A. Scarano, eds. *Colonial Crucible: Empire in the Making of the Modern American State.* Madison: University of Wisconsin Press, 2009.

Ninkovich, Frank. *The United States and Imperialism.* Malden, Mass.: Blackwell, 2001.

Tyrrell, Ian, and Jay Sexton, eds. *Empire's Twin: U.S. Anti-imperialism from the Founding Era to the Age of Terrorism.* Ithaca, N.Y.: Cornell University Press, 2015.

LEGAL AND CONSTITUTIONAL ISSUES

Burnett, Christina Duffy, and Burke Marshall, eds. *Foreign in a Domestic Sense: Puerto Rico, American Expansion, and the Constitution.* Durham, N.C.: Duke University Press, 2001.

Margolies, Daniel S. *Spaces of Law in American Foreign Relations: Extradition and Extraterritoriality in the Borderlands and Beyond, 1877–1898.* Athens: University of Georgia Press, 2011.

Raustiala, Kal. *Does the Constitution Follow the Flag? The Evolution of Territoriality in American Law.* New York: Oxford University Press, 2009.

Sparrow, Bartholomew H. *The Insular Cases and the Emergence of American Empire.* Lawrence: University Press of Kansas, 2006.

AN AGE OF EMPIRE: THE WORLD IMPERIAL SYSTEM ON THE EVE OF WORLD WAR I

Belich, James. *Replenishing the Earth: The Settler Revolution and the Rise of the Anglo-World, 1783–1939.* New York: Oxford University Press, 2009.

Darwin, John. *The Empire Project: The Rise and Fall of the British World-System, 1830–1970.* New York: Cambridge University Press, 2009.

Go, Julian. *Patterns of Empire: The British and American Empires, 1688 to the Present.* New York: Cambridge University Press, 2011.

Hochschild, Adam. *King Leopold's Ghost: A Story of Greed, Terror, and Heroism in Colonial Africa.* New York: Houghton Mifflin, 1999.

Rosenberg, Emily S., ed. *A World Connecting, 1870–1945.* Cambridge, Mass.: Belknap Press of Harvard University Press, 2012.

Zimmerman, Andrew. *Alabama in Africa: Booker T. Washington, the German Empire, and the Globalization of the New South.* Princeton, N.J.: Princeton University Press, 2010.

THE SPANISH-CUBAN-AMERICAN AND PHILIPPINE-AMERICAN WARS

Hoganson, Kristin L. *Fighting for American Manhood: How Gender Politics Provoked the Spanish-American and Philippine-American Wars.* New Haven, Conn.: Yale University Press, 1998.

Linn, Brian McAllister. *The Philippine War, 1899–1902.* Lawrence: University Press of Kansas, 2000.

Miller, Bonnie M. *From Liberation to Conquest: The Visual and Popular Cultures of the Spanish-American War of 1898.* Amherst: University of Massachusetts Press, 2011.

Pérez, Louis A. *The War of 1898: The United States and Cuba in History and Historiography.* Chapel Hill: University of North Carolina Press, 1998.

Schoonover, Thomas. *Uncle Sam's War of 1898 and the Origins of Globalization.* Lexington: University Press of Kentucky, 2003.

Tone, John Laurence. *War and Genocide in Cuba, 1895–1898.* Chapel Hill: University of North Carolina Press, 2006.

CUBA

Ferrer, Ada. *Insurgent Cuba: Race, Nation, and Revolution, 1868–1898.* Chapel Hill: University of North Carolina Press, 1999.

Guridy, Frank Andre. *Forging Diaspora: Afro-Cubans and African Americans in a World of Empire and Jim Crow.* Chapel Hill: University of North Carolina Press, 2010.

Helg, Aline. *Our Rightful Share: The Afro-Cuban Struggle for Equality, 1886– 1912.* Chapel Hill: University of North Carolina Press, 1995.

Pérez, Louis A., Jr. *Cuba in the American Imagination: Metaphor and the Imperial Ethos.* Chapel Hill: University of North Carolina Press, 2008.

HAWAI'I

Kauanui, J. Kēhaulani. *Hawaiian Blood: Colonialism and the Politics of Sovereignty and Indigeneity.* Durham, N.C.: Duke University Press, 2008.

Merry, Sally Engle. *Colonizing Hawai'i: The Cultural Power of Law.* Princeton, N.J.: Princeton University Press, 2000.

Okihiro, Gary Y. *Island World: A History of Hawai'i and the United States.* Berkeley: University of California Press, 2008.

Silva, Noenoe K. *Aloha Betrayed: Native Hawaiian Resistance to American Colonialism.* Durham, N.C.: Duke University Press, 2004.

THE PHILIPPINES

Anderson, Warwick. *Colonial Pathologies: American Tropical Medicine, Race, and Hygiene in the Philippines.* Durham, N.C.: Duke University Press, 2006.

Delmendo, Sharon. *The Star-Entangled Banner: One Hundred Years of America in the Philippines.* New Brunswick, N.J.: Rutgers University Press, 2004.

Go, Julian, and Anne L. Foster, eds. *The American Colonial State in the Philippines.* Durham, N.C.: Duke University Press, 2003.

Ileto, Reynaldo C. *Filipinos and Their Revolution: Event, Discourse and Historiography.* Manila: Ateneo de Manila University Press, 1998.

Kramer, Paul A. *The Blood of Government: Race, Empire, the United States, and the Philippines.* Chapel Hill: University of North Carolina Press, 2006.

May, Glenn Anthony. *Social Engineering in the Philippines: The Aims, Execution and Impact of American Colonial Policy, 1900–1913.* Westport, Conn.: Greenwood Press, 1980.

Salman, Michael. *The Embarrassment of Slavery: Controversies over Bondage and Nationalism in the American Colonial Philippines.* Berkeley: University of California Press, 2001.

Shaw, Angel Velasco, and Luis H. Francia. *Vestiges of War: The Philippine-American War and the Aftermath of an Imperial Dream, 1899–1999.* New York: New York University Press, 2002.

PUERTO RICO

Ayala, César, and Rafael Bernabe. *Puerto Rico in the American Century: A History since 1898.* Chapel Hill: University of North Carolina Press, 2007.

Briggs, Laura. *Reproducing Empire: Race, Sex, Science, and U.S. Imperialism in Puerto Rico.* Berkeley: University of California Press, 2002.

del Moral, Solsiree. *Negotiating Empire: The Cultural Politics of Schools in Puerto Rico, 1898–1952.* Madison: University of Wisconsin Press, 2013.

Findlay, Eileen J. *Imposing Decency: The Politics of Sexuality and Race in Puerto Rico, 1870–1920.* Durham, N.C.: Duke University Press, 1999.

Monge, José Trías. *Puerto Rico: The Trials of the Oldest Colony in the World.* New Haven, Conn.: Yale University Press, 1997.

OTHER CARIBBEAN OCCUPATIONS

Gobat, Michel. *Confronting the American Dream: Nicaragua under U.S. Imperial Rule.* Durham, N.C.: Duke University Press, 2005.

Greene, Julie. *The Canal Builders: Making America's Empire at the Panama Canal.* New York: Penguin Press, 2009.

Langley, Lester D. *The Banana Wars: United States Intervention in the Caribbean, 1898–1934.* Revised ed. Wilmington, Del.: Scholarly Resources, 2002.

Renda, Mary A. *Taking Haiti: Military Occupation and the Culture of U.S. Imperialism, 1915–1940.* Chapel Hill: University of North Carolina Press, 2001.

Veeser, Cyrus. *A World Safe for Capitalism: Dollar Diplomacy and America's Rise to Global Power.* New York: Columbia University Press, 2002.

CONNECTIONS ACROSS IMPERIAL SITES

Baldoz, Rick. *The Third Asiatic Invasion: Empire and Migration in Filipino America, 1898–1946.* New York: New York University Press, 2011.

Bender, Daniel E., and Jana K. Lipman, eds. *Making the Empire Work: Labor and United States Imperialism.* New York: New York University Press, 2015.

Chang, Kornel. *Pacific Connections: The Making of the U.S.-Canadian Borderlands.* Berkeley: University of California Press, 2002.

Gonzalez, Juan. *Harvest of Empire: A History of Latinos in America.* New York: Viking Press, 2000.

Jacobs, Margaret D. *White Mother to a Dark Race: Settler Colonialism, Maternalism, and Indigenous Child Removal in the American West and Australia, 1880–1940.* Lincoln: University of Nebraska Press, 2009.

Merleaux, April. *Sugar and Civilization: American Empire and the Cultural Politics of Sweetness.* Chapel Hill: University of North Carolina Press, 2015.

Poblete, Joanna. *Islanders in the Empire: Filipino and Puerto Rican Laborers in Hawai'i.* Urbana: University of Illinois Press, 2014.

Sneider, Allison L. *Suffragists in an Imperial Age: U.S. Expansion and the Woman Question, 1870–1929.* New York: Oxford University Press, 2008.

BUSINESS

Ayala, César J. *American Sugar Kingdom: The Plantation Economy of the Spanish Caribbean, 1898–1934.* Chapel Hill: University of North Carolina Press, 1999.

Colby, Jason M. *The Business of Empire: United Fruit, Race, and U.S. Expansion in Central America.* Ithaca, N.Y.: Cornell University Press, 2011.

Hart, John Mason. *Empire and Revolution: The Americans in Mexico since the Civil War.* Berkeley: University of California Press, 2002.

O'Brien, Thomas F. *The Revolutionary Mission: American Enterprise in Latin America, 1900–1945.* New York: Cambridge University Press, 1996.

Rosenberg, Emily S. *Financial Missionaries to the World: The Politics and Culture of Dollar Diplomacy, 1900–1930.* Durham, N.C.: Duke University Press, 2003.

Soluri, John. *Banana Cultures: Agriculture, Consumption, and Environmental Change in Honduras and the United States.* Austin: University of Texas Press, 2005.

IMPERIAL CULTURE

Brody, David. *Visualizing American Empire: Orientalism and Imperialism in the Philippines.* Chicago: University of Chicago Press, 2010.

Hoganson, Kristin. *Consumers' Imperium: The Global Production of American Domesticity.* Chapel Hill: University of North Carolina Press, 2007.

Hunter, Jane. *The Gospel of Gentility: American Women Missionaries in Turn-of-the-Century China.* New Haven, Conn.: Yale University Press, 1984.

Kaplan, Amy. *The Anarchy of Empire in the Making of U.S. Culture.* Cambridge, Mass.: Harvard University Press, 2002.

Mendoza, Victor Román. *Metroimperial Intimacies: Fantasy, Racial-Sexual Governance, and the Philippines in U.S. Imperialism, 1899–1913.* Durham, N.C.: Duke University Press, 2015.

Reeves-Ellington, Barbara, Kathryn Kish Sklar, and Connie A. Shemo, eds. *Competing Kingdoms: Women, Mission, Nation, and the American Protestant Empire, 1812–1960.* Durham, N.C.: Duke University Press, 2000.

Rydell, Robert W. *All the World's a Fair: Visions of Empire at American International Expositions, 1876–1916.* Chicago: University of Chicago Press, 1984.

Tyrrell, Ian. *Reforming the World: The Creation of America's Moral Empire.* Princeton, N.J.: Princeton University Press, 2010.

Index